T0356993

THE
LAST
MOB
LAWYER

THE LAST MOB LAWYER

TRUE STORIES FROM THE MAN WHO DEFENDED SOME OF THE BIGGEST NAMES IN ORGANIZED CRIME

BRUCE H. NAGEL, Esq. and
S. M. CHRIS FRANZBLAU, Esq.

Forefront
BOOKS

The Last Mob Lawyer: True Stories from the Man Who Defended Some of the Biggest Names in Organized Crime
Copyright © 2025 by S. M. Chris Franzblau and Bruce H. Nagel

All rights reserved. No part of this publication may be reproduced, stored in a retrieval system, or transmitted in any form by any means, electronic, mechanical, photocopy, recording, or otherwise, without the prior permission of the publisher, except as provided by USA copyright law.

No patent liability is assumed with respect to the use of the information contained herein. Although every precaution has been taken in the preparation of this book, the publisher and author assume no responsibility for errors or omissions. Neither is any liability assumed for damages resulting from the use of the information contained herein.

Published by Forefront Books, Nashville, Tennessee.
Distributed by Simon & Schuster.

Library of Congress Control Number: 2024926650.

Print ISBN: 978-1-63763-427-1
E-book ISBN: 978-1-63763-428-8

Cover Design by Bruce Gore, Gore Studio, Inc.
Interior Design by PerfecType, Nashville, TN

Printed in the United States of America

DEDICATION

To my brother, Jimmy, who shared my dreams and my soul and always was there for me.

CONTENTS

CONTENTS

FOREWORD

When I started out as a young trial attorney in the New York metropolitan area, everyone talked about a handful of legal legends. Those were names that made their way into just about every interesting, shocking, and/or hilarious trial story my generation of lawyers talked about. And considering the area we worked in, there had been *plenty* of those kinds of cases over the past fifty years.

At the top of that list of legendary lawyers was Chris Franzblau. I swear, I saw his name connected to just about every past case that got my attention. Those were largely mob cases involving a laundry list of colorful characters who were deeply connected in the world of organized crime. Meyer Lansky. Jerry Catena. Anthony "Tony Pro" Provenzano. Jimmy Hoffa. Simone "Sam the Plumber" DeCalvacante and

Salvatore "Sally Bugs" Briguglio. Whenever I heard or read Chris's name, I knew it was a case I'd want to learn more about.

Imagine how it felt, then, the first time I realized I had *the* Chris Franzblau as my opposing counsel on a civil case.

Was I thrilled to see him in action?

Was I terrified of facing off against a guy who had achieved near-mythical status in New York and New Jersey legal circles?

The answers to those two questions, in order, are *yes* and *hell yes.*

More than anything, though, I saw it as a challenge.

This was my chance to knock this big shot off his perch, to bring the local legend back down to earth. And I came out swinging.

The start to our professional relationship was anything but professional. It was ugly. It quickly became apparent to both of us that neither was going to back down—*ever.*

We butted heads all through that case . . . and through many subsequent cases. We had nasty, insulting interactions. One time in a deposition, he came around the table and got right in my face. The threat was more than implied. His steely-eyed stare communicated strength and bravado earned from decades of going toe-to-toe with mobsters. It didn't hurt that he looked like someone straight out of central casting for *The Godfather.*

For twenty years, neither Chris nor I ever said one nice word to the other. And we were both perfectly happy with the terms of our relationship.

Then, sometime around 2010, we were both guests at the wedding of a mutual friend at the Plaza Hotel in Manhattan. Late in the evening, after we'd all enjoyed a lovely ceremony, a wonderful meal, and a few drinks, our host, Steven Katz, brought us together. Out of respect for him, we obliged.

"Chris, Bruce," he said, "it's time to end all this nonsense between the two of you. It's over. It's done. Now, I want you to bury the hatchet once and for all."

"Where?" I asked without hesitation. "In his forehead?"

There was a split second of silence, none of us certain what would happen next.

Then I saw a smile break through Chris's gruff exterior.

I laughed.

He laughed.

We shook hands, and we've been good friends ever since. He's even honored me by joining my law practice as a senior litigator at age ninety.

Several years ago, just after Chris turned eighty-five years old, I became mildly obsessed with the idea of saving his treasure trove of stories and memories for posterity. I said, "Chris, you aren't getting any younger. When you're gone, we are going to lose all your incredible stories. They'll be lost forever. I cannot let that happen, so we're going to start an oral history. The world cannot lose everything you've experienced over the past eighty-five years."

So, over the next few years, Chris and I had several video recording sessions. Actually, those weren't "recording sessions" as much as they were an opportunity for me to sit back and marvel at some incredible cases and historical events this man has lived through. Cameras captured story after story about the top mobsters of the fifties, sixties, and seventies and about the intersection of organized crime and politics, entertainment, business, and culture.

This book is our effort to record a small group of those stories and to share them with the world.

The stories you're going to read are all true. They were written by me from Chris's perspective, just as he has told them to me over the years. He's also been very active in the development of this book, and he has personally reviewed and signed off on every chapter, offering corrections and additions whenever needed.

Believe it or not, as I sit here writing this fore-word, today is Chris's ninety-third birthday. I actually just drove him home a few hours ago from a little cel-ebration we had for him. We had a great chat in the car, just as we always do. His sharp mind continues to amaze me.

It's hard to imagine a day when I won't be able to sit down with him and laugh together as he tells (and retells) all these now-familiar stories in person. But when that day finally comes, I'll at least be able to pour myself a drink and turn the pages of *The Last Mob Lawyer.*

And now, so can you.

Bruce Nagel

October 2024

INTRODUCTION

I'm a mob lawyer.

I spent more than forty years of my legal career representing some of the most notorious men in the history of organized crime. But today, writing this at age ninety-three, I've managed to outlive all the mob bosses, hit men, enforcers, con artists, bag men, capos, and empty suits who filled my days with contracts and pretrial motions and my nights with a strange mix of excitement and anxiety.

You might say I'm the last man standing of a bygone era of gangsters, mafiosos, and civilized brutality.

Some highlights from throughout my storied career include

- representing the head of the Genovese crime family and arguing for his freedom in front of the United States Supreme Court after he was incarcerated for refusing to answer questions before the New Jersey State Crime Commission.

- representing the International Brotherhood of Teamsters (known as the Teamsters) in its heyday under Jimmy Hoffa, and knowing why he was killed and where he really is buried.

- representing Anthony "Tony Pro" Provenzano and his notorious hit man Sal Briguglio, who was linked to fifty murders. (Briguglio was gunned down in Little Italy the day before he was to meet me to prepare for his trial for the murder of a Teamster rival to Tony Pro.)

- witnessing a raging fight between Jimmy Hoffa and Tony Pro in the visitor's room at Lewisburg Penitentiary, in which each vowed to kill the other and their family— even their pets.

- watching the mob save the careers of Frank Sinatra and Tony Bennett.

- fighting the extradition of "the Mob's Accountant," Meyer Lansky, from Israel, where he fled in 1970 to avoid criminal prosecution.

- meeting at the Beverly Hills Hotel with Las Vegas mob boss Moe Dalitz, who had planned the escape of my Genovese crime family boss client before his subpoenaed appearance before a Los Angeles grand jury.

- representing Simone "Sam the Plumber" DeCavalcante after the FBI had illegally wiretapped his New Jersey office for almost two years and then released the tapes publicly to blunt the backlash after their other illegal wiretapping operations—including those against Dr. Martin Luther King Jr. and Muhammad Ali—were revealed to the public.
- playing golf with Kirk Douglas, Sam Klein (a major shareholder in Bally's), and the Genovese boss at La Costa Resort in California—a round of golf that resulted in the ultimate divestiture of Klein's shares in Bally.
- representing the mob owners of the Havana Riviera in Cuba to recover the assets lost following Castro's violent takeover.

The Talking Heads once sang, "I've met the people you read about in books." For decades, this line served as my personal mantra. Few people can say they were at the center of the key agreements and interactions among some of the world's most famous (and infamous) attorneys, organized crime figures, entertainers, politicians, and business magnates. It often felt like I was living within the pages of a gripping novel, never quite sure what would happen on the next page. The characters seemed larger than life, and, in my work as an attorney, the stakes were incredibly high. Conversations that might seem unbelievable to most people became commonplace to me. Whether it was in the courtroom or at a high-profile dinner or event, I was privy to many encounters that sent ripples across the nation. Nearly every day, I was watching history being written.

Over my nine decades on this earth, I've come to realize that those figures, though villainized and mythologized in the media, were not as easily understood as you might expect. Things weren't always clearly black or white, good or bad. Those individuals were complex. They were shocking in their brutality *and* in their generosity. They were notoriously cruel *and* surprisingly kind. They were just as likely to cut you *down* as they were to cut you *in*. They were driven by the same desires, fears, and ambitions as you or me—but their actions reverberated longer and louder than most of ours.

Looking back, I see that I was given an education in human nature, power, and the forces that shape our world. The people I met, especially my clients, will forever be etched in my memories, shaping my mindset and becoming a part of my legacy, just as they've become a part of America's legacy.

Some of it good.

Most of it bad.

In the pages ahead, I'll take you on a journey through my career working with these "made men." This isn't an autobiography nor a detailed history of organized crime in America. It's a handful of memories from an interesting career, a collection of real-life stories I thought I'd share with you rather than taking to the grave with me.

This is merely a snapshot into the life of America's last mob lawyer.

Enjoy.

Chris Franzblau
October 2024

CHAPTER 1

The Early Years

I was a kid of the Great Depression, born and raised in 1930s New Jersey. Ours was one of the few Jewish families in a predominantly Irish neighborhood. My father was an attorney, so we didn't have it quite as bad as many other Jersey families back then, but times were still tight. My young mind couldn't fully appreciate the harsh realities of the Great Depression that ravaged the world outside our small but comfortable single-family house in Newark. It wasn't until much later that I realized it was the bank, not my parents, that really owned our home. Apparently, even a practicing attorney couldn't withstand the financial pressures and foreclosures of the day.

My father was my hero nonetheless. He was successful, respected, brilliant, handsome, charismatic, and an incredible athlete. Dad was also a veteran, having enlisted in the army at age seventeen near the end of World War I. If he had been just a year or two older and had been able to join the war effort much earlier, there's a good chance he never would have made it home to start a family. I can picture him racing into the heat of battle, bravely facing down enemy fire to serve his country and protect his brothers-in-arms. That's the kind of man he was. A hero.

After the war, Dad came home and went straight to law school without ever attending college. Sounds crazy today, but it was possible back then. He excelled in his studies and passed the bar exam at an impressive twenty years of age after only two years of law school. He finished so quickly, in fact, that he had to wait around for several months after passing the bar before he could be sworn in. The minimum age for becoming a member of the bar was twenty-one.

My dad was my mentor and my protector, and I was always with him—and often with his clients—at social functions, on the golf course, and at Ruppert Stadium on Saturdays to see the old Newark Bears play baseball in the International League. I went everywhere with him. He also loved the theater and music, and he would take me to shows and concerts regularly and kept a library of poetry at home for my sister and me.

I thought he was invincible, and he gave me a feeling of security that stayed with me my entire life. Later, when I became a father of three, I always tried to raise my children the way he raised me.

That strong, constant, fatherly influence was critical to me growing up because my mother wasn't always available to us. She suffered from crippling depression and was occasionally hospitalized and seldom left the house. So again, Dad stepped up as a father and as a husband. He took care of the house, shopped for groceries, bought our clothing, and took my mother on the Hoboken Ferry several days a week for her appointments with a prominent psychiatrist in New York City.

Even though Dad never made a lot of money, he still managed to join a local golf club, where he taught me to play. My favorite thing to do when I was in high school was to play a round with him at the Crestmont Golf Club in West Orange, New Jersey. I never could have guessed at the time how important those regular games would be to my career as an attorney myself.

One of my regular golfing buddies in the late 1950s was Abner "Longie" Zwillman, a well-known and highly respected Jewish businessman—and a member of an organized crime family in New York. My father knew Zwillman long before I did, though.

They fought Nazis together.

In New Jersey.

Literally.

When German sympathizers organized in Newark, Irvington, Watchung, and other New Jersey cities with large German populations in the late 1930s, Zwillman assembled a group of ex-boxers, tough guys, and some of his thugs to break up the Nazi-friendly meetings . . . and break their Nazi-friendly bones. The group included notorious men such as the Halper brothers, the Hye brothers, Max Arno, Big Soo Katz, and Red DeCesare. Not everyone in this band of pro-America warriors was part of the mob, however. Prominent businessmen and attorneys—including my father—joined Zwillman's campaigns against Nazi sympathizers in our communities.

It might shock you to hear about a group of mobsters beating back the tide of Nazi Germany on the streets of Jersey. As you'll see throughout this book, most of the people I've known in organized crime are not *all* bad *all* the time. They were complicated men with complicated motivations. Oftentimes, their biggest motivators were protecting their family and communities; other times, their motives weren't quite as noble.

My father died in 1963 at the age of sixty-two. I was devastated. In an age when fathers often kept their children at arm's length and left the child-rearing to the mothers, my dad was all in. No one knew me better than my father. Even now, more than sixty years after his passing, I can still hear his voice cheering me on and telling me how proud he is of me every day.

COLLEGE AND LAW SCHOOL

After high school, I attended Muhlenberg College in Allentown, Pennsylvania, a fine Lutheran school that required church attendance three days a week. Despite being one of a small handful of Jewish students enrolled, I faithfully attended every church service and excelled at the college's required Bible classes.

After three years, however, I grew bored with school and decided to enlist in the military. It was 1952, and the Korean War was raging. Most of my friends from high school were being drafted into service, and I felt uneasy staying in school, safe and bored, while my peers were being shipped off to war. My father had enlisted as soon as he was legally able to during WWI. Who was I to do any less?

Dad, however, was heartbroken about my decision to leave school without a degree. He saw great potential in me even when I couldn't see it in myself. I had never really enjoyed school, and I had grown to loathe college. A legal career had never been on my radar at all. However, before I could drop out and enlist, my father conspired with the head of the religious studies program at Muhlenberg, who was close friends with the dean of Duke Law School. Duke required entering law students to have a college degree, but the dean graciously decided to make an exception for me.

"Look," the dean told my Bible professor, "if the kid passes high enough on the law aptitude test, I'll admit him without a college degree." I'm sure the law school dean never expected me to actually *pass* the test, let alone score highly enough to force him to follow through on his promise.

But I did.

And *he* did.

Believe it or not, that's how I went to law school.

Though I wasn't sure about it at first, it didn't take long for me to see the wisdom in my father's and religious studies professor's intervention. I quickly fell in love with studying the law, and I made lifelong friends at Duke. I was elected president of our class in my second and third year at Duke and was a member of the university class council. I even planned to teach law upon graduation.

My golf skills opened many doors during my law school years as well. Both the dean of the law school and my constitutional law professor—the former solicitor general of the United States under President Franklin D. Roosevelt—learned I was an accomplished golfer and invited me to join them regularly at their country club. As our golfing relationship developed, they began inviting me into their homes for dinner and other social events, which opened many doors for me even before I completed my law degree. These contacts proved valuable throughout my studies and well into my career.

In what felt like the blink of an eye, I finished law school and in 1955 passed the bar exam in Washington, DC; New York; and New Jersey. By then, though, I was fed up with education and my years and years of nonstop studying. I was ready for some action. So I did what I had planned to do three years earlier: join the military. Only this time, I'd be joining as an attorney.

THE NAVY

I quickly learned that I wasn't done with my education after all. When I joined the navy, I went straight into Officer Candidate School in April 1956, which was brutally tough. I became extremely close with the twenty-four guys in my class at Newport, Rhode Island, and felt that I had finally become ready for any physical or mental challenge after completing that rigorous training program. I got a huge break soon after, as I was given top secret clearance by the FBI and attended the US Navy's cryptography school for top-secret coding and decoding. This gave me a certain status among naval officers. After completing that program, I was assigned to the Naval Justice School for studying the Uniform Code of Military Justice to be qualified to conduct courts-martial and other legal responsibilities for whomever I was to be assigned in the future.

My first assignment was to Naval Air Station in Pensacola, Florida. This was the second biggest break of my life.

Upon arrival, it was customary to present yourself to be formally introduced to the commanding officer and to receive your assignment. When I arrived at Admiral Loomis's office, his aide told me that the admiral was not there. I thanked him and turned to leave when the aide asked a question that would literally define my entire naval career.

"Wait a sec," he said. "Any chance you know how to play golf?"

An hour later, I was at the Pensacola Officers Golf Club playing with the admiral, the chief legal officer, and the commanding officer of the Marine Corps barracks. It was a remarkable and unexpected opportunity to spend time with the top leaders, and I was determined not to squander it. We had such a good time that afternoon that these high-ranking men became my weekly golfing crew. We played at the club every weekend for the duration of my stay in Pensacola. I also traveled with the admiral regularly to many other bases, always playing golf with him on these trips at some of the best courses in the country. The famous Blue Angels were in our command at Pensacola, so I even golfed and flew all over the country with them as well.

I became the admiral's special liaison, and as such I traveled first class on US naval planes wherever I went. Although I was primarily an assistant legal officer, I presided over the officers' dining room, and dinner could not begin without my approval. I was also put in charge of the brig, a job that came in quite handy in ingratiating myself to my superiors. I had the authority to put minor violators on work detail, so I began to send men out to work on the traps and landscaping at the golf club. This became a regular practice, something that the members of the Officers Club noticed and greatly appreciated.

During my time in Pensacola, I often flew with the admiral to the Guantanamo Bay naval base in Cuba, which was under the command of the Pensacola navy commanding officer. Havana in 1957 was a bustling place with two gambling hotels, The Nationale and Havana Riviera. The Copacabana Casino was also an exciting establishment, welcoming people from all over at that time. The hotels and casinos were magnificent in their decor and atmosphere, women were elegantly dressed, the flourishing restaurants and shops were inexpensive but luxurious, and everyone was there to have fun. The culture in Havana was an eye-opener.

A man named Mike Leon from New Jersey was an investor in Havana Riviera, along with Meyer Lansky and several other mobsters from Canada. When Castro came out of the hills and began taking over the country in 1958, however, the Riviera was

confiscated by the new government and all the investors lost everything.*

Many years later, I represented Mike Leon and
other investors before the United States Claims
Commission in Washington to try to recover the lost
investments in Cuba. The judgments I obtained can
be collected only when the United States recognizes
Cuba, and I am sure that the heirs of the clients I represented have no idea those judgments may someday
be worth a fortune.

Near the end of 1958, I requested a transfer to
Naval Station Norfolk in Virginia to be closer to my
father, whose health was gradually fading. I arrived
a couple of days before Christmas and volunteered
to take watch for Christmas and New Year's Eve.
Because I'm Jewish, working on Christmas was no big
deal to me, and it gave me a chance to make a good
first impression on my new commanding officer.

At midnight on Christmas Day, I was awakened
by the chief petty officer, who informed me that there
was an emergency at the main entry gate to the base.
I raced to the scene and found a *very* intoxicated
base commanding officer and a young, injured sailor

---

* Claims were filed in the United States for reparation if and
when domestic relations with Cuba resume.

lying on the ground. The admiral had enjoyed a bit too much "Christmas cheer" and had hit the sailor with his car, knocking the victim off his motorcycle. The local police were on the way, so I had to act fast. I put the sailor in a navy ambulance headed to the hospital, and I had the admiral driven home before the local authorities arrived. Needless to say, my new commanding officer appreciated my efforts, and that incident laid the foundation for what would become an excellent relationship during my time at Naval Station Norfolk.

ADJUSTING TO CIVILIAN LIFE

I left the navy soon after arriving in Norfolk and returned home to join my father's law practice while I explored other opportunities for my post-military career. It wasn't long before I was appointed to the US Attorney's Office in Newark as an assistant US attorney in the Criminal Division. Dwight Eisenhower was president, and William Rogers was his attorney general.

As an assistant US attorney, I tried many criminal cases and obtained my share of convictions. However, as a Republican appointee, I was replaced in 1962 when John F. Kennedy, a Democrat, became president. I took a job with a small law firm in Newark, and even though I wasn't there very long, joining that little firm changed the entire trajectory of my career. It was there that I had my first big criminal case—the one that first opened the door to what would become decades of defending some of the biggest names in organized crime.

CHAPTER 2

My First Criminal Clients

My first real mob case came to me in 1963. I'd been let go from my job as assistant U.S. attorney with the change of administration. I took a job at a small firm and, though I wasn't there long, that is where I landed my first big criminal case. For a younger lawyer like me, it was a fairly notorious beginning.

My client was a jeweler named Hy Chuven, who had trafficked, or fenced, about 170,000 platinum ingots that someone else had allegedly stolen from Engelhard Industries, one of the world's largest smelters of precious metals. Authorities had him dead to rights, but Chuven wasn't who the prosecutors really wanted. Instead, they were after Harold "Kayo" Konigsberg, the man they suspected of actually stealing the ingots.

Konigsberg had a reputation as an enforcer for the Mafia—and an even worse reputation for being a nasty, difficult man with a violent streak. He was also a semipro heavyweight boxer at about 265 pounds and six foot three. This, in addition to having *K* and *O* as the first two letters of his last name, was how he got his nickname Kayo, as in KO or "knockout." It was one he had entirely earned.

Konigsberg delighted in hurting people. He was notorious, but not because he was high up in any single prominent Mafia family. Instead, he was unique in that he had a working relationship with *many* of them.

He made his money through a number of unsavory means, including bookmaking and hijacking, but his real focus was on moneylending, or loan-sharking. And he always made it clear to his clients that he won whether they paid him back or not. If they did, he made more money. If they didn't, he got to do what he loved most in the world: hurt people.

The prosecution wanted Chuven to inform on Konigsberg. They really applied the pressure to my client, but I counseled him not to rat out Kayo. I didn't see enough of an upside for him to take that risk. Without Chuven's testimony, the prosecution's case came up short and both Chuven and Konigsberg, whom I'd never even met, were acquitted.

It was my first major criminal defense case and my first criminal defense victory—a great start to my new career as a defense attorney.

I was at that small firm for only a few months before my father suffered a stroke, leaving him completely incapacitated. Without a moment's hesitation, I left my new job and took over my father's practice to make sure his clients were taken care of, the bills were paid, and that we could close the practice well. After all he'd done for me, there was no way I was going to let him down when he needed me most.

My wife also became very ill around that time, which added to my stress and growing list of responsibilities.

Dying father, sick wife, leaving my job twice within a year, closing down my father's law practice . . . it was an emotional time for me, and keeping all the plates spinning kept me busy 24-7. It was uncommon for most people to work on weekends in those days, but I was putting in a lot of hours at Dad's practice and spent plenty of Saturdays alone in the office. That's where I was one Saturday morning when my work was disturbed by an unexpected, heavy knock at the door.

Imagine my surprise when I opened it to find none other than Harold "Kayo" Konigsberg. He was an imposing man with big fists, a torso like a keg, and a heavy jaw. He wore his hair in a pompadour. He practically filled the entire doorframe.

"Do you recognize me?" he asked.

Of course I did.

"Yeah, I know who you are," I said.

"How do you know?"

"From the newspapers. And from when I was in the US Attorney's Office. Of course, I know who you are."

Obviously, I also knew him because I'd just represented Chuven in the platinum ingots case. I knew he knew that, and I figured that's how he knew me too.

What I didn't know was why he was standing in front of me, filling the entire doorway—or how he knew to find me in my father's office, alone, on a Saturday morning.

I couldn't help but feel intimidated, but I wasn't panicked. Despite his reputation, I couldn't imagine why Konigsberg would have been upset with me. After all, I was the one who had counseled Chuven not to testify against him. I figured he owed me for that, a belief that kept what would have otherwise been perfectly reasonable terror at bay. Besides, I was curious to hear what he had to say.

He got right to the point.

"I was just indicted," he said. "Me and some other guys. I'd like you to represent one of them."

"What happened?" I asked.

"We were indicted for possession of stolen property."

I'd come to learn that Konigsberg always spoke plainly and with little emotion. No matter the subject, he was straightforward, telling me his sordid antics with the same matter-of-fact tone he'd use to describe the weather. He didn't embellish, he didn't over-explain, and he wasn't a great storyteller. He stuck to the cold, hard facts nine times out of ten. We went on to have other conversations over the years in which he'd open up a bit more, and I was shocked to see what an intelligent man he was. He never graduated from high school and was practically illiterate, but he had a near-photographic memory and a deep knowledge of American history. I doubt any of his mobster friends ever knew how incredibly smart Konigsberg really was.

In that first encounter, though, Kayo kept things simple, factual, and surface level. Understandable. He didn't trust me . . . yet.

I was intrigued and took the case, which turned out to be a hijacking of high-end menswear, specifically Hickey Freeman clothes coming out of Canada, where they were manufactured. I represented one of Konigsberg's colleagues, Stacy Giuliano, and I'm afraid it didn't go all that well. Giuliano was convicted. In fact, they all were.

Before my client could be sentenced, however, I got a phone call informing me that he was dead. He and Konigsberg had had an argument during the trial, and the authorities later found his body floating in Manhattan Bay. I never learned for certain what happened after their fight, but I could make an educated guess. Giuliano picked a fight with a mobster who loved to hurt people. Two plus two almost always equals four.

Konigsberg had been out on bail for the hijacking case as well as an extortion rap, in addition to three others, when Giuliano was killed. That fall, Kayo finally reported to prison to begin his sentence. The first thing he did was bribe the warden to ensure he'd live a lavish life behind bars for the next few years. When he was released, he moved to a retirement community in Florida, irritating his neighbors by paying off most of the staff in exchange for special treatment and privileges that no one else enjoyed. I guess you can take the mobster out of Jersey, but you can't take Jersey out of the mobster.

My involvement with both Chuven and Konigsberg was the first step in what would become a long career as a criminal defense attorney handling some of the highest profile clients in the country.

Every young trial attorney strives to make a name for himself and dreams of handling cases involving household names and celebrities. In my case, though, the celebrities were famous for all the wrong reasons. They were the most notorious mobsters, union leaders, businessmen, and politicians in the country.

It's kind of ironic that my career as a defense attorney got started with the theft of a truckload of precious metals—because my involvement with Chuven and Konigsberg was pure gold.

CHAPTER 3

The Notorious Tony Pro

O ne of the most infamous, multifaceted figures
I ever represented was Anthony Provenzano,
known to his associates as "Tony Pro." That's a name
you'll see often throughout this book.

Tony Pro had come up during the Great Depression as a truck driver in New York City, and he joined
the Teamsters Union. He started working his way up
the ranks, becoming a shop steward by 1941 and boss
and president of the Teamsters Local 560 in 1958.

Tony was always suntanned, well groomed, and
well dressed in expensive suits, with a sparkling diamond ring on his pinky. At that time, he was fairly
heavy, maybe 220 pounds, though he was not very
tall. Later on in life, he would get very into fitness and

was in much better shape. He was a bright and highly effective union negotiator, charming and persuasive when he wanted or needed to be.

He commanded respect from union members all over the country, and he got it.

Tony loved his job as the head of the Teamsters Local 560. You might even say he'd kill to keep that position.

You *might* say that.

See, years before I met him, Tony was challenged for his union leadership position in 1961 by Anthony Castellito, the Local 560 secretary treasurer, who was supported by a union faction that was intent on reform. The faction had demands, including stopping extortion of money from member companies and halting sweetheart contracts.

Tony Pro was making a very good salary as president—nearly as much as Jimmy Hoffa, the Teamsters International president—and he had plans to skim a lot more. Given all that was at stake, he didn't want to lose that election. And since Tony just happened to be a lieutenant in the Genovese crime family, he had the power, the means, and the disposition to have his rival eliminated.

The first man he hired for the job was a familiar name to me: Kayo Konigsberg. Salvatore "Sally Bugs"

Briguglio and Salvatore "Big Sal" Sinno, an imposing figure who often served as Tony's bodyguard, rounded out the crew.

The hit was planned and, with the arrangements settled, Tony flew to Florida. Believe it or not, he was actually getting married there while his enforcers took care of Castellito. What better alibi could there be than being out of state at your own wedding when the crime took place?

On the morning of June 5, 1961, Castellito parked outside of the Local 560 office. Big Sal walked up to him and told him that Tony Pro had a friend who needed to hide out from the authorities for a few days. He asked if the friend could use Castellito's country house in Kerhonkson, about two hours north of Manhattan. Castellito agreed. After all, he wanted to stay friendly with Tony Pro.

Who wouldn't?

The two of them got into Castellito's car and drove to pick up Tony's "friend" who needed a place to hide. One of Kayo's associates played the role to perfection. Not suspecting the trap, Castellito rode with them to the country house.

When they walked inside the house, Sally Bugs came out of hiding and hit Castellito in the back of the head with a lead pipe. When a still-conscious

Castellito began to fight back, Kayo ripped a cord off some venetian blinds, wrapped it around Castellito's neck, and choked the life out of him.

Kayo buried the body about 140 miles away.

The following week, Kayo showed up at Tony Pro's office for his $15,000 payment. Kayo threw his arm around Tony's shoulders and kissed him on the cheek. Tony Pro handed him the envelope approvingly, saying, "Very good."

With his challenger, Castellito, out of the way, Tony was comfortably reelected president of Local 560. Castellito's disappearance remained a mystery for the time being, and Tony's star within the Teamsters was rising high. In addition to securing his role as the local union president, he had recently been promoted by Jimmy Hoffa to vice president of the Teamsters International. His promotion happened even after the feds, who had been watching the union with court-appointed monitors, ordered Hoffa to fire him because of his corrupt activity.

Even Robert Kennedy himself, who was head of the Justice Department under his brother's presidency, had Tony Pro in his sights. But Hoffa relied on Tony Pro's connections to the mob to provide him with muscle and influence. With Hoffa's friendship, and with his position in the union solidified, Tony Pro was in a good spot.

However, as good as he had it, Tony must have felt some details of the Castellito coverup were unresolved, and he decided to tie up (or cut off) those loose ends. He knew he could trust Sally Bugs, but he wasn't so sure about Big Sal Sinno and Kayo Konigsberg.

Tony never paid Big Sal what he promised him for the job—a decision that would come back to bite Tony Pro later on. For the time being, though, Big Sal had disappeared. Tony had no idea where or how to find him, and it'd be nearly fifteen years before he'd turn back up. I'll get back to that in a later chapter.

Kayo, however, was a very front-and-center concern. He was a major player in the area, and Tony Pro didn't like someone like Konigsberg having that much leverage over him. So he decided to take Kayo out.

Not long after Castellito's murder, Tony set up an ambush for Konigsberg at the Cabana Club, one of several clubs that Kayo had taken over as payment for unpaid loans. Despite being shot four times, Kayo survived and escaped by barricading himself in the kitchen before sneaking out the window and fleeing.

Before Tony Pro could try again, someone higher up the ladder decreed that Kayo was not to be touched. They believed the services he provided to the organization were too valuable. That left Tony Pro in an awkward position, as Kayo knew Tony was responsible for the failed hit.

About a year later, it seemed that Tony's mishandling of the Kayo Konigsberg situation nearly cost him his life. A janitor found Tony's moaning, semiconscious body at the bottom of an elevator shaft in a four-story office building the Teamsters owned in Union City. Those in the know made it clear that Kayo had pushed Tony down the elevator shaft. It's not hard to imagine, given Kayo's love of violence—and, of course, the fact that Tony tried to have him killed.

Tony was in the hospital for months recuperating from severe injuries, but he eventually recovered and things appeared to get back to "normal." I'm not sure if he and Konigsberg ever repaired the rift between them after that.

• • •

I first met Tony Pro in the early 1960s at the Englewood Country Club, when I was fresh out of the US Attorney's Office. I'd just golfed with a friend, and we went to the club lounge for a drink. My friend saw

Tony Pro, whom he already knew, and we walked over to say hello.

Tony was sitting there with Sally Bugs Briguglio, his right-hand man, and Vito Genovese—the boss of the Genovese family (who would soon be headed to prison for conspiring to import and sell narcotics).

We joined the group for drinks, spending most of our time talking about golf. That chance encounter and friendly chat was a memory that would stay with Tony Pro for years. That was a lucky break for me, because it meant Tony would remember me years later when a mutual friend recommended me to represent him.

I was reintroduced to Tony Pro by David T. Wilentz, one of the most highly regarded attorneys in New Jersey. Wilentz had spent a decade as the New Jersey state attorney general from 1934 to 1944, and he had successfully prosecuted the infamous Lindbergh baby kidnapping case. He was a major member of the Democratic National Committee and a powerful voice in Democratic politics. Wilentz was also a friend of my father, and I was good friends with his son.

Hy Zoloto, a politically successful New York lawyer and power broker, contacted David Wilentz on behalf of Tony Pro.

He explained, "We need a lawyer who's familiar with the federal criminal statutes and some labor law."

Wilentz said, "I know just the guy." He arranged a dinner for Zoloto, himself, and me, and it went well. They recommended me to Tony, who remembered me from our encounter at Englewood, and he hired me. Tony was personally represented by Zoloto, who was handling his appeal on a recent racketeering conviction, and I was brought on to represent the pension plans for all the Teamsters unions in New Jersey.

That was a great time in my life. I was in my midthirties, fairly young in my law career, and glad for the job representing the Teamster pension plans. It was a prestigious case and paid very well.

In time, of course, I'd learn more about who Tony Pro truly was. But early on, I knew him primarily as a man with a friendly, outgoing way about him and a cadre of loyalists, including his brothers Nunzio and Sal, and, of course, Sally Bugs. I'd heard some stories about his mob connections, but I didn't know for sure what was fact and what was fiction. Back then, Mafia personnel and activity were not as commonly known as they are now; it was much easier to control the flow of information in those days.

As for "what I knew and when I knew it" when I started working for him, I'll say that I certainly knew

Tony was facing the extortion charge, but I mainly knew him not as a criminal but as a well-respected union leader. And I did not know until many years later that, by the time I started working with Local 560, Tony had already committed the crime that would end up sending him to prison for the rest of his life.

CHAPTER 4

Enter Jimmy Hoffa

Today, Jimmy Hoffa is a name surrounded by myth and mystery. The people *loved* the famed union boss—almost as much as the government hated him. He was seen by many as a modern-day Robin Hood and by others as a mobster thug, and his sudden disappearance in 1975 sparked a thousand conspiracy theories people are still making documentaries and writing about fifty years later.

Working with Tony Pro on Teamsters Union business didn't just put me on Jimmy Hoffa's radar—it literally put me in his office.

Much like Tony Pro, Jimmy Hoffa was a renowned figure in both union leadership and organized crime. Unlike Tony, Jimmy was always dressed conservatively.

They both dressed well, but Tony Pro was a good bit *flashier.* He liked cashmere topcoats, expensive suits, and luxury brands. Jimmy Hoffa, on the other hand, was more of an off-the-rack kind of guy, picking nice-looking but much more modest brands.

Hoffa also had a much different lifestyle than most of the people in Tony Pro's circle. You might even say he was *squeaky clean.* He didn't drink or womanize, and he had an almost religious devotion to his daily exercise routine, which he had scheduled down to the minute. That man worked, and he worked hard. And he was always a union guy. Even as a teenager in Indiana, long before getting involved with the Teamsters, he helped organize and empower the workers in a grocery store.

It is no exaggeration to say Jimmy Hoffa was all business, and he was good at what he did. He did not like wasting time, and he could get very impatient. Tony Pro prepared me ahead of time before my first meeting with him, and the protocol was always the same. When you have a meeting with Jimmy Hoffa, you get there early (never, *ever* show up late), and then you shake hands, sit down, talk business, and get out. Hoffa didn't do small talk. He didn't care about your weekend plans or how your family was doing. If you were lucky enough to make it onto his calendar, your job was to squeeze every last drop of business productivity you could out of the time you had together.

The first time I met Hoffa, Tony Pro and I were in DC for meetings in the beautiful Teamsters offices about important national contract negotiations Hoffa and Tony Pro were working on together.

It was a tense time for Jimmy Hoffa and the Teamsters. Robert F. Kennedy, then the attorney general of the United States, was bringing the full weight of the Justice Department down on Hoffa, and the investigation was generating a lot of bad press. After John F. Kennedy won the presidency and named his brother attorney general, RFK turned up the heat on organized crime in general—and on Jimmy Hoffa in particular.

RFK had made it his personal mission to expose Hoffa and the criminal infiltration of trade unions. He had been investigating Hoffa since 1957, grilling him in front of the Senate's bipartisan Rackets Committee, as it was called, but Hoffa had remained cool even as Kennedy was visibly frustrated. Kennedy charged Hoffa at various points with bribery, fraud, and misuse of the pension fund. But all that negative attention didn't affect Hoffa's popularity or his power.

At that time, nearly a third of American workers belonged to a union. The Teamsters Union had about a million truck drivers and warehouse workers, and Jimmy Hoffa was the public face of the whole union movement. He kept getting reelected to his leadership position, and the union kept growing robustly. Hoffa was unflappable, and he never let the pressure of the many investigations break him, at least publicly. As he once said, "All my life, I've been under investigation."

That's not to say Hoffa was laid-back or took all the investigations in stride, however. The truth is, he hated RFK as much as RFK hated him—maybe more so. He hadn't let Kennedy get the best of him yet, though, but none of us was sure how long that luck would hold.

The day Tony and I were in his office, Hoffa showed a little of the anger he worked so hard to mask in public. There was a big plate glass window behind his desk overlooking a huge Washington, DC, park. Right across the park sat the Justice Department buildings, including the offices of the attorney general.

We were sitting there talking when, all of a sudden, Hoffa turned around in his chair and gestured out the window.

"You see those buildings over there?" he said to me. "That's where Robert Kennedy is, the guy who hates me and is trying to hang me. That's where his office is. You might as well take a good look at it."

The meaning was clear. Hoffa wanted us to know the face of the enemy.

Another time, Hoffa, Tony Pro, and I traveled to New York City for labor negotiations with a company there. We negotiated all day and then went to the Luxor Turkish Baths with Hy Zoloto.

The Luxor was a beautiful old hotel featuring Renaissance-style architecture, with nine stories aboveground and two below. It was a place where celebrities such as Tennessee Williams and big shots like Barney Balaban, the president of Paramount, could be found getting massages alongside regular guys. Besides the baths, it had a large swimming pool, a club, a gym, a barbershop, and even a podiatrist.

You name it, they had it.

It took Jimmy Hoffa about thirty seconds to spot the one thing they *didn't* have, though: a union.

Hoffa struck up a conversation with the guy giving him his rubdown. He learned that the Luxor had about a hundred employees to keep it running in tip-top shape, from the clerks checking you in to the Russian masseuses rubbing you down. By the end of Hoffa's massage, he'd organized the employees of the Luxor. Even lying naked on a massage table, Jimmy Hoffa couldn't stop doing union work.

Like I said, he didn't believe in wasting time.

CHAPTER 5

Ol' Blue Eyes and the Mob

I traveled with Tony Pro often during my years representing him and the Teamsters, but nearly all our trips were confined to the state of New Jersey, with the occasional flight to DC to meet with Jimmy Hoffa. A few times, though, we needed to head west to address Tony's union interests in the up-and-coming town of Las Vegas.

The whole Vegas experience was still relatively new in those days. They had started building hotel-casinos in the 1950s, and they hadn't stopped. Vegas's tourism ramped up exponentially every year, and all the glitz, glamour, and traffic was concentrated into a relatively small path through the heart of the city that would become known as the Strip.

In the early days, the crowning jewel of the Las Vegas Strip was the Sands Hotel and Casino. Visitors today might see the Sands as relatively modest compared to the newer, more audacious hotels that crowd the Vegas skyline, but in that era, the Sands was simply magnificent.

I spent quite a bit of time at the Sands over the years, handling not only Tony Pro's union business but also representing the Sands directly on occasion. The staff came to recognize me, and Aaron Weisberg, who ran the hotel, usually put me up in a suite when I was in town.

I'll be honest: It was a pretty sweet gig.

As a kid who'd grown up during the Great Depression, walking through the Sands made me feel like I was strolling through the streets of heaven. There was a bustling casino, incredible shops, white-gloved restaurants, a beautiful pool, and well-to-do people who were laughing while spending loads of cash from end to end.

And the celebrities! The great crooners from the glory days were always belting out their classics live and in person, and the world's most famous actors could be found both onstage and in the casino. Frank Sinatra, Dean Martin, Sammy Davis Jr.,

Peter Lawford, Joey Bishop . . . it's no wonder why the original 1960 film *Ocean's 11* was filmed right there in the Sands—all the actors were there all the time anyway!

A lot of those guys were . . . allegedly . . . friendly with high-ranking mob figures. I won't blow the whistle on them, but I can share at least one story that shows how commonplace it was for guys in the mob to rub shoulders with Hollywood's finest.

The stories about Sinatra's ties to the mob are mostly true, but his familial connection to organized crime somehow flew under the radar for most of his life. Ol' Blue Eyes himself was the godson of Willie Moretti, the one-time underboss of the Genovese crime family and a cousin of former mob boss Frank Castello.

If you've seen *The Godfather*, you probably remember the scene in which Michael tells Kate about how his father sent Luca Brasi to a bandleader to get Johnny Fontaine released from his contract. What you don't know is that this scene was inspired by Willie Moretti's relationship with Sinatra. Moretti, Sinatra's real-life godfather, got him released from his contract with Tommy Dorsey by jamming a gun down Dorsey's throat.

"I'm giving you one dollar to release Frank from his contract," Moretti told a gagging Dorsey. "Take it."

Moretti was nothing if not a tough negotiator.

Willie Moretti had many celebrity friends in Sinatra's social circle, including Dean Martin and Jerry Lewis. In fact, Willie Moretti was supposed to have lunch with Lewis at Joe's Elbow Room in Cliffside Park, New Jersey, on the very day he was murdered by a mob hit man.

That in itself was an interesting story. Moretti had contracted syphilis. Now, that sounds bad enough on its own, but it became an even bigger issue for this once-respected gangster. Moretti's syphilis had begun to affect his cognitive function. That is, it had begun to destroy his brain, impairing his judgment and making him unpredictable. And if there's one thing the mob doesn't like, it's an impaired, unpredictable mind filled with decades of mob secrets.

Afraid he'd *unburden* himself to the authorities, bosses ordered a hit on Moretti.

Notorious triggerman Albert Anastasis of Murder, Inc. was believed to have taken out Sinatra's godfather. It was such a high-profile hit, I've always been surprised that the press, which loved to theorize about

Frank Sinatra's mob connections, never reported this, his most significant one.

I might have asked Sinatra about this myself—if I'd ever had the chance to meet him. The closest I ever got was hearing his voice behind his dressing room door.

At least, that is, when the stars weren't worried about being seen with their more seedy friends and associates.

One night, Tony Pro and I were in town for some meetings, and we decided to see Sinatra's show. That in itself was unusual for me. I didn't usually attend the shows; I preferred to spend my free time golfing. But that night, we saw Sinatra.

After the show, Tony asked me if I wanted to meet Sinatra. The union's original offices were in Hoboken, where Sinatra grew up, and he and Tony knew each other from earlier years.

Who wouldn't want to meet Ol' Blue Eyes at the height of his fame?

So off we went backstage, and Tony knocked on the door. Sinatra's guy comes to the door—big, tall, and imposing.

"We're here to see Sinatra," Tony Pro said, showing zero hesitation or intimidation.

"Who are you?" the guy asked.

"Tony Pro."

"Wait here," he said and went inside. We stood there in the hall for a while, and finally Sinatra's man returned.

"I'm sorry to tell you, Mr. Pro, but Mr. Sinatra can't see you now," he said, and shut the door.

Tony was outraged—and probably more than a little embarrassed. He was used to his name *opening* doors, not getting them literally slammed in his face.

He yelled through the door at the goon who had disrespected him. He yelled at Frank Sinatra, who was no doubt standing within ten feet of us. He banged on the door with his fist. But that was it. The door did not reopen, and no one bothered to reply to Pro's protest.

Tony and I stood awkwardly in the hall for a minute or two, and then we left. It was one of the most uncomfortable moments I ever spent with him. A big part of my job was to keep him happy. I knew all too well what could happen when he wasn't.

We got word later that Sinatra was in negotiations to buy a casino in Las Vegas at the time, and he was having some problems with the Gambling Control Commission. He was being investigated, and he couldn't afford to be seen laughing it up with known mobsters such as Tony Pro. That would have just brought more scrutiny and doubts to the deal Sinatra was trying to make in town.

Tony Pro wasn't used to being turned away. I'm sure he understood the reasoning behind Sinatra's snub, but I am curious what their next conversation sounded like.

Regardless, that's the story of how I *almost* met Frank Sinatra.

CHAPTER 6

Standing Up to Sally Bugs

In my work as the lawyer for Local 560 and other local unions, I was responsible for the unions' pension plans. It was my job to keep them safe, clean, and on the level. These funds represented the retirement hopes and dreams of every union member in my community, and I took that responsibility seriously.

But that wasn't always easy.

While I was neck-deep in the Local 560's fund, I didn't have anything to do with the Teamsters International pension fund. That one was a whole different ballpark—a park, it turned out, that a lot of people were playing in all the time.

International's fund was big. It grew right along with union membership, and membership was on the rise in those days. But those funds were always being picked apart by several different Mafia families who routinely used the pension fund as their own personal bank. They'd pull huge sums out of the fund as "loans" they'd then use to fund various businesses. It was common for a chunk of union pension money to go to a casino or to union bosses such as Jimmy Hoffa, who'd then use the cash to grease the palms of officials who needed paying off.

Oftentimes, these loans were not paid back promptly, which caused the funds to miss out on market growth. Other times, the loans were not repaid at all. The whole situation was a mess, and I had my hands full trying to keep everyone's grubby fingers out of the smaller funds I was responsible for. I wanted to keep my workers' pension safe. Plus, I wanted to avoid the investigations that always plagued the International fund.

One time, my efforts to do that almost cost me my life.

I was attending a board meeting at the Teamsters convention in Wildwood, New Jersey. A union pension fund is run by a board of trustees made up of three or more people from management and three from the union, so a convention can be a convenient time to have a meeting since all the required people are present for convention business.

At this particular meeting, Sally Bugs presented a loan deal to the board. A group of developers from Detroit wanted to use Teamster money to build a project called Lauderhill, near Fort Lauderdale, Florida. They wanted an approximately $8 million mortgage for a vacant apartment building, which they wanted to turn into time-shares, and Sally Bugs wanted it approved.

I looked over the documents, and I saw the names of these guys from Detroit. As I read, it occurred to me that this might be organized crime over there. I was reading between the lines, and I knew it wasn't a good loan. My job was to protect that pension fund, not to blindly approve however anybody wanted to use it.

So I said no.

"This loan is doomed," I said to the board.

Sal pushed back. Hard. He really wanted it, and he brought all the weight of his enforcer anger down on me for denying the deal. But I didn't give in or waver, no matter how mad he got with me.

"Look," I said. "We're not taking that mortgage. It just doesn't make sense for this pension plan to take that mortgage in Florida."

The discussion went around the table, and then it came back to Sal again. He looked at me with those cold, calculating eyes. "Chris, you're here to give us legal advice. Don't be making business judgments for us."

I responded, "I'm telling you outright, I will not give any legal approval, and I wouldn't touch closing that mortgage in a million years."

"Look, I told you before," he said to me, "don't give us business advice. Otherwise, you just might not wake up in the morning. Sometimes, people don't, ya' know?"

I don't remember thinking much about my next words. If I had, I probably would have said things differently. I would have remembered what kind of guy I was talking to. I might have thought about all the people Sally Bugs was believed to have killed.

Instead, the words just flew out of my mouth without a moment's hesitation.

"Let me tell you something. You can take your gun and shove it up your ass."

The room went dead quiet as Sal considered what to do next.

After a few moments, chatter resumed, and the board continued to discuss Sal's proposal while I considered whether I really would wake up the next morning.

I'd be lying if I said I didn't breathe a sigh of relief when my alarm woke me the next day.

Sally Bugs paid me a visit a few days later. He was there to apologize. At first, I figured Tony Pro had gotten wind of the argument and had spoken to Sal. Looking back now, though, I think there was more to it than that.

By that time, while I was still representing the Teamsters Union pension fund, I had taken on a new client by the name of Jerry Catena. Jerry had built an empire through vending machines, pinball machines, trucking, and gambling. I'd known him since I was a teenager, and he and my father had been good friends, making Jerry more like family to me. Oh, and did I mention Jerry was also the boss of the Genovese crime family?

Considering how I'd spoken to Sally Bugs, I'm pretty sure my relationship with Jerry Catena saved my life that week. Getting revenge for a little back talk from me wasn't worth calling down the full force of the Genovese family.

Despite my objection, the pension board approved Sal's proposal to extend a mortgage for the property in Florida.

The deal blew up quickly thereafter, just as I knew it would. The builders were indicted and went to trial in Fort Lauderdale. The presiding judge, Alcee Hastings, was later impeached by the US Senate and subsequently lost his judgeship in 1989. And what was the impeachable offense? He accepted a bribe by one of the parties in Sally Bugs's terrible time-share project. He went on to run for a congressional seat in the US House of Representatives in 1992—a position he held for nearly thirty years until his death in 2021.

Like I told Sal and the board, that whole deal was doomed from the start. In the end, it lost millions of dollars from the pension fund, cost a federal judge his judgeship, and almost got me killed.

But at least I had the satisfaction of being proved right—and, of course, of telling a murderous mob enforcer where he could shove his handgun.

CHAPTER 7

The Bill Comes Due for Tony Pro and Jimmy Hoffa

For most of my association with Tony Pro, he was on what you might call borrowed time. He was indicted in 1960 for extortion and racketeering for receiving payoffs from the Dorn Transportation Company throughout the 1950s. He was found guilty in 1963, but he had high hopes of getting off on appeal.

I started representing the Local 560 pension fund soon after his conviction. The guilty verdict surprised him; I'm told he didn't seem to take the whole trial all that seriously. At one point, his own lawyer even had to ask the judge to make him answer the questions put to him!

The conviction also came without the testimony of what would have been a key witness for the prosecution. Walter Glockner, a union member and truck driver for Dorn, was scheduled to testify to all sorts of illicit activity in the union organization Tony Pro ran. However, Glockner got into a fight with one of Tony's relatives in a union meeting the week before his scheduled appearance in court.

The next morning, someone shot and killed Glockner outside his home.

When the press asked Tony about the murder, he said, "I loved the guy. He looked just like my son. Those dimples. That smile. I practically raised him. I saved his job I don't know how many times. He was accident-prone."*

Maybe Glockner *accidentally* fell into the path of those oncoming bullets?

Tony Pro was sentenced to seven years in prison for the Dorn extortion conviction, but he was allowed to delay his incarceration until after he'd exhausted his appeals. That time came nearly three years later, in May 1966, when he finally had to surrender himself

---

* "Labor: Tony Pro Takes a Tumble," *TIME*, June 21, 1963, https://time.com/archive/6812606/labor-tony-pro-takes-a-tumble/.

to begin his sentence. He was sent to the Lewisburg Federal Penitentiary in Pennsylvania, where I visited him many times.

Though he was behind bars, Tony Pro was never without friends and business associates. Lewisburg became the temporary home for a lot of mob figures, including Tony's Teamsters boss, Jimmy Hoffa, whose luck ran out soon after Tony's.

In May 1963, Hoffa was found guilty of bribing a grand juror in connection with his 1962 trial for conspiracy. Like Tony Pro, Hoffa stayed out on bail throughout the full appeal process. During that time, he was convicted again of conspiracy and defrauding the Teamsters' pension fund, which added five more years to his original eight-year sentence. He began his prison term at Lewisburg in March 1967, just ten months after Tony Pro arrived there.

Though they'd had a friendly affiliation for many years, serving time together soured their relationship. The breaking point may have been Hoffa's refusal to help Tony Pro regain his $1.2 million union pension, which he was forced to forfeit upon his conviction. Hoffa had managed to retain his own pension due to statutory differences, and that disparity never sat well with Tony. When Hoffa declined to help Tony Pro get his pension back—money he felt he had more than earned for his hard work on behalf of the Teamsters— Tony was enraged.

Given each man's stubbornness and temper, their strained relationship was bound to come to blows at some point. I guess it's just dumb luck that I happened to be there to see it.

I was with Tony in the prison's visiting room one afternoon. Hoffa was there as well, taking other visitors. Before I knew it, the two men were arguing, then screaming, and then full-on brawling. They had a raging fight, right there among other prisoners, visitors, and several correctional officers.

I heard both of them make vicious threats at each other.

One yelled, "I'm gonna kill you, you son of a bitch!"

The other replied, "Yeah? Well, I'll kill you, your whole family, and your damn pets!"

Between blows, Hoffa yelled, "It's because of people like you that I got into trouble in the first place!"

This further enraged Tony Pro, who took the "people like you" as a slur against Italian Americans.

It was like something out of a movie. It happened almost sixty years ago, but I can still see the whole fight play out in my mind like it was yesterday. Hell,

I'm nearly a hundred years old, and I've still never seen anything like it.

Whenever I visited Tony after that, I would often also see Hoffa on the other side of the visiting room meeting with his own attorneys. Fortunately, the visiting room was quite large, and the two men were able to peaceably keep their distance. After their brawl, they each decided it would be best for everyone if they just ignored each other for the rest of their stay at Lewisburg Federal Penitentiary.

As an attorney, I was also fascinated by the other famous—or *infamous*—inmates I saw at Lewisburg while visiting Tony Pro. Perhaps the most interesting was Colonel Rudolph Abel, a Russian spy who had been arrested for gathering US intelligence and sending it to Russia. Years later, after the American pilot Francis Gary Powers was shot down in his U-2 spy plane while doing reconnaissance over Soviet airspace, our government exchanged Abel for Powers. (The story was later made into the movie *Bridge of Spies* starring Tom Hanks.)

. . .

Tony Pro was paroled in November 1970, after serving four and a half years of his seven-year sentence. Jimmy

Hoffa was released a year later, in December 1971, after serving not quite five years of his thirteen-year sentence. His release didn't *just happen*, however. It certainly wasn't luck. Instead, Hoffa made his own luck by paying Attorney General John Mitchell half a million dollars to get Nixon to pardon him. When he did that, though, Hoffa had no idea that his pardon would come with a ban preventing him from further union activities.

He was furious when he got this news.

He didn't intend to abide by this ban, of course. Immediately upon his release, he started trying to regain his position as Teamsters president. He fought the ban in court and worked behind the scenes to shore up support in the union. By that time, the union had about 2.2 million members, and he must have felt he built it all by himself. He was certainly still beloved by most members.

Meanwhile, Frank Fitzsimmons had stepped into the Teamsters president position. Fitzsimmons allowed the mob to siphon off hundreds of thousands of dollars from the pension fund to pay for organized crime projects and line mob pockets. Everyone was happy with this arrangement, and no one wanted Hoffa to come back in and mess things up.

Undeterred, Hoffa made himself into a huge nuisance to the mob throughout the early 1970s. He started speaking publicly about the need to cut organized crime out of union business. As if that weren't bad enough, he also made it clear that, if he weren't allowed to run for reelection, he might just have to "unburden" himself to the feds of everything he knew about the mob and the greedy fingers they kept sticking into the Teamsters' pension funds.

That may have been the last straw. Maybe it was something else entirely. After all, he had racked up a long list of enemies over the past forty years. Regardless, by the summer of 1975, the mob decided Jimmy Hoffa was too much of a risk to leave walking the streets.

Few people in the know were surprised, then, when Hoffa disappeared on July 30, 1975. He was living in the Detroit area at the time, and he left his home that day to attend a meeting with none other than Tony Pro.

Hoffa never showed up.

He was never seen again, and the question, "What happened to Jimmy Hoffa and where is his body?" remains one of America's greatest unsolved mysteries.

Actually . . . I should say it remains one of America's greatest *officially* unsolved mysteries. Some people do know what happened, but no one has ever been charged in that case. The investigation into Hoffa's disappearance remains open to this day.

In a strange coincidence, the answer to this mystery lies at the intersection of the two authors of this book. Bruce Nagel and I have both known part of the story for decades. Imagine our surprise when we put our pieces together!

It was common knowledge that Tony Pro and his hit squad, led by Sally Bugs Briguglio, had carried out many contract killings for the Genovese family. The informed word on the street was that Sally Bugs and two other Local 560 business agents, the Andretta brothers, carried out the hit on Jimmy Hoffa and dumped his body on a construction site in New Jersey.

The government began a thorough investigation, throughout which I represented Tony Pro and Sal Briguglio. No hard evidence against them ever surfaced.

The *New York Times*, however, got a tip from an anonymous eyewitness who claimed to have seen a few men bury a body inside an oil drum on a New Jersey construction site owned by mobster Brother Moscato. The *Times* ran an article detailing what they'd heard, in which they reported that the FBI had, in fact, searched the Moscato property, but their search had come up empty.

The body was never found.

Even though the FBI's search of the Moscato property did not turn up Hoffa's body, I can confidently say from personal knowledge that whoever called the *Times* with that tip *almost* got it right. I'm told the body *is* at that location (though not in a drum) and that the feds were looking in the wrong spot. They missed it by about one hundred yards!

How do I know this?

It turns out there *was* an eyewitness to the secret disposal of Jimmy Hoffa's body—and amazingly, that witness had been the college roommate of my coauthor, Bruce Nagel!

Bruce told me about an incredible conversation he had with his friend and former roommate, Jeff, in 1978. Bruce had graduated from Cornell University in 1974, and Jeff graduated in 1975, just a couple of months before Hoffa's disappearance. After graduation, Jeff took a summer job working for his father, who was a major contractor working a job in Jersey City on the exact site mentioned in the *Times* article.

Jeff's duties included sitting on top of a perch and counting the number of trucks coming in and out of the job site and keeping track of all the materials that were dumped there. One afternoon, he said a man he didn't know approached him, handed him a twenty-dollar bill, and told him to go eat lunch somewhere off-site for an hour or so. Jeff explained that he was pretty sure this guy was a mobster just by the way he dressed and spoke. A bit uneasy about the situation, Jeff did as he was told, leaving his observation perch unattended. However, curiosity got the best of him, and he snuck over to another vantage point to see what was going on.

From there, Jeff saw two cars with Michigan plates drive onto the construction site. They parked, and he watched as men emerged from a black Cadillac, opened the trunk, and pulled out what he was certain was a human body wrapped in a sheet. The men dropped the body in a fill area and covered it with lime. Then they got back in their vehicles and drove away.

That night, Jeff told his father what he'd seen.

His father looked at him with steely eyes and said, "Son, you are never to speak of this again—*ever*. Not to me, not to your friends, not to *anyone*."

"Why, Dad?" he asked.

"Because you're probably the only person alive who knows exactly where Jimmy Hoffa is buried."

Jeff followed his father's advice for a while, but after his dad died in 1978, he felt a bit freer in sharing this wild story. Sometimes, the truth is so good it simply *has* to come out!

CHAPTER 8

The Castellito Conspiracy Roars Back to Life

Refusing to back Sally Bugs on the terrible Florida apartment building investment ended my tenure as the attorney for Local 560—and, as I've said, it could very well have ended my life. Sal Briguglio was not someone you wanted as an enemy. But despite the dustup during the pension board meeting, and even though my work for the union was over, my employment by Sally Bugs himself was just beginning.

In 1975, the murder of Anthony Castellito, Tony Pro's rival in the 1961 Teamsters presidential election, was ancient history. No one had ever been charged, and it had probably been a decade since Tony Pro or Sal Briguglio had even thought about it.

Remember from chapter 3, Tony Pro had organized the hit, which was carried out by Sally Bugs, Kayo Konigsberg, and Salvatore "Big Sal" Sinno. In the aftermath, Tony tried (and failed) to have Konigsberg killed. He also never paid Big Sal, who disappeared soon afterward and hadn't been seen or heard from for about fourteen years. I'm sure he saw what happened to Kayo and decided he'd be safer somewhere else.

In 1975, we all learned where that "somewhere else" was when Big Sal returned—with a vengeance.

Literally.

Apparently, Sal Sinno had fled New Jersey to a town near Milwaukee, Wisconsin, where he'd been working for the railroad under an alias. He'd been in a relationship with a woman for a while, and they had two kids together. One night, the couple got into a terrible argument that ended with Big Sal hitting her.

She did not like that. Not one bit.

To get back at him, she called the Hoboken, New Jersey, police department. And boy, did she have a story to tell them.

She explained to the Hoboken authorities that a man living under the name of Charles Caputo in Fond du Lac, Wisconsin, was actually Salvatore Sinno, who was wanted for "some serious crime" in Hoboken.

Police didn't react right away, though, and she didn't say anything about it to Sinno.

A couple of weeks later, when the phone bill arrived, he noticed the outbound call to a New Jersey phone number and figured out what she'd done. In a panic, Sal called the one guy he'd been hiding from for all these years—Tony Pro. He was hoping to get back into Tony's good graces so Tony would help him disappear again.

Tony was surprisingly gracious when he got the phone call. He wired Big Sal $2,500 and promised another $2,500 if he came to get it in person. Smelling a setup, Sinno declined and instead called the FBI, asking to be put into witness protection in exchange for information about his former mob associates. After all, he had something he knew they wanted: the truth about what had happened to Anthony Castellito.

The feds were faster on the uptick than the Hoboken police, and they jumped at the chance to get a valuable Mafia informant. They put Sinno back into hiding and brought murder charges against Tony Pro, Kayo Konigsberg, and Sal "Sally Bugs" Briguglio.

Tony Pro retained Murray Edelbaum, a New York attorney who was well known for defending organized crime figures. Konigsberg was already in prison on another charge, and he was represented by Ivan Fisher, one of the top criminal defense lawyers in the country. And Sally Bugs Briguglio, who had threatened my life years earlier in the pension fund board meeting, retained me.

The trial was set to begin on the Tuesday after Easter in 1978. I set up a meeting with Briguglio to prepare for court for the Friday before, which was Good Friday. I waited, but he never showed up for that meeting.

Later that day, I learned that Sally Bugs Briguglio had been shot and killed as he walked out of Umberto's Clam House in Little Italy.

The word on the street was that he had been spotted walking into the US Attorney's Office in Newark. Despite his long history as Tony Pro's trusted, go-to enforcer, the mob was not going to risk Briguglio spilling his guts to the feds about his involvement with Tony Pro and all his mob friends. He simply knew too much. *Way* too much.

On June 14, 1978, Tony Pro and Konigsberg were convicted of killing Castellito.

As expected, Big Sal Sinno served as the star witness for the prosecution. He disappeared again into witness protection after the trial, but that wasn't the last we heard of him. Ten years later, Sinno was back in the headlines when he was arrested in New York City after shooting an acquaintance on the street in 1988.

Konigsberg appealed his conviction and won the right to a new trial. For some reason I'll never understand, though, Kayo chose to represent himself in the retrial.

He lost.

That leaves my longtime friend and client, Anthony "Tony Pro" Provenzano. After a long and illustrious career with the Teamsters and with the mob, his luck finally ran out, bringing an end to the notorious Tony Pro's illegal activities.

In 1978, he was sentenced to twenty-five years to life for his role in the murder of Anthony Castellito. And once the dominoes started to fall, they didn't stop.

A month later, he was sentenced to four years for arranging kickbacks on a $2.3 million pension fund loan. One year after that, he was convicted on labor racketeering charges, which landed him another twenty-year prison term.

He went to prison for the last time in 1978 at the age of sixty-one.

Tony Pro spent the next ten years behind bars. On December 12, 1988, he died of a heart attack at Lompoc Federal Penitentiary in Lompoc, California, at the age of seventy-one.

CHAPTER 9

Jersey's Silent Ruler:
The Rise of Jerry Catena

The Prohibition era was a launching pad for several of the mob's biggest names, and Newark was the undisputed epicenter of New Jersey's organized crime. The streets of Newark were littered with speakeasies—shadowy enclaves where you could get a drink away from the prying eyes of authorities and the menace of rival gangs. Privacy and secrecy were paramount in these establishments, which were governed by one simple rule: If the bartender didn't recognize you, you weren't getting in. Period.

Bootlegging—the illegal production and distribution of alcohol during Prohibition—created vast underground networks and generated massive profits for those involved. Several key players emerged and became prominent figures in organized crime. One of the top dogs was Abner "Longie" Zwillman, who controlled up to 40 percent of all illegal liquor traffic in the United States from 1926 to 1933, smuggling much of it into the country along the Jersey coast. Other big names included Louis Holtz, Sam Reinfeld, and of course Gerardo "Jerry" Catena, who would become perhaps my most notorious client.

These bosses were a generation removed from me. I worked with some of them in their later years, but I knew them even as a boy. My father was friendly with many of them.

Bootlegging was serious business in the early days of the mob. "Lucky" Luciano, the founder of the modern American Mafia, and Meyer Lansky, a key architect of organized crime in the United States and a major figure in the development of the National Crime Syndicate, led a Jersey-based bootlegging group.

Lansky knew Zwillman and brought him into Lucky Luciano's New Jersey operations. He quickly rose through the ranks and was recognized as a sig nificant player by the late 1940s. Zwillman was even called out by name as a key leader by the Kefauver

Committee, the first government committee assembled to expose the enormity of organized crime in the early 1950s.

Longie Zwillman led a network that included many young and ambitious associates, including rising star Jerry Catena. As a young lieutenant, Catena was well connected with notable mob figures like Luciano and Lansky. Hailing from Newark, Catena followed in Zwillman's footsteps by establishing himself in the trucking business—a common front for illegal activities such as smuggling and hijacking—and the longshoreman's union, which provided control over the waterfront and opportunities for various rackets, including extortion and theft.

When Prohibition ended, Zwillman also brought Catena on as a partner in one of his most profitable businesses, Runyon Sales Company, which distributed vending machines and gaming equipment, items commonly used in illegal gambling operations.

Catena made a name for himself through these ventures and was well placed to step into higher and higher levels of leadership as they became available. His biggest break happened right after World War II, when Lucky Luciano, the head of the American Mafia, was deported to Italy. Frank Costello briefly took over the family, but he soon relinquished control to Vito Genovese after a too-close-for-comfort assassination attempt believed to have been orchestrated by Genovese convinced him to "retire."

When Vito Genovese officially took over, the Luciano family became known as the Genovese family. Genovese appointed Jerry Catena as his underboss, mob-talk for second-in-command. This cemented his place in the hierarchy of organized crime.

In 1957, Catena accompanied his boss, Vito Genovese, to the notorious "Apalachin Meeting." The meeting was held at Apalachin, New York, home of Joseph "Joe the Barber" Barbara, capo of the Buffalo crime family. The purpose of the meeting was to solidify Genovese's position as boss and to seek the blessing of other mob leaders for Carlo Gambino's takeover of the New York mob after the murder of its former leader, Albert Anastasia.

Having all the key players from the New York and New Jersey mob under one roof was a huge risk—and one that almost destroyed everyone's operations. The meeting's secrecy was compromised when the New York State Police became suspicious of the numerous out-of-state cars parked at the Barbara residence. When the police began creeping around writing down license plate numbers, Joseph Barbara's wife alerted the attendees. This created an explosion of chaos, and many of the attendees fled through the woods.

Reportedly, sixty men were arrested out of the estimated one hundred in attendance. They were convicted of obstruction of justice for refusing to explain the meeting's purpose, but these charges were later overturned on appeal. Nonetheless, the damage was done. This disastrous meeting exposed the American Mafia's existence and shattered any illusion that the Mafia was a mere myth, as FBI Director J. Edgar Hoover had long maintained.

Vito Genovese was eventually imprisoned, which significantly increased Jerry Catena's influence within the Genovese family. Tasked with overseeing New Jersey operations, Catena quickly became a cornerstone of the Genovese empire.

• • •

I first met Jerry Catena long before his rise to power. As I've mentioned, my father was friendly with Longie Zwillman and Jerry Catena, and the three of them would often golf together. I remember meeting

Catena in the late 1940s, when I was in my teens. I spent a lot of time golfing with my father at the Crestmont Country Club in West Orange, so it was certainly no surprise to bump into his other golfing buddies when we were enjoying a round together.

Many years later, after I'd begun my legal career, a mutual friend recommended me to Catena when he needed representation. We hit it off well enough, and that began an attorney-client partnership that would last more than forty years.

I found Catena to be quiet, soft-spoken, and private, always avoiding public attention. He was married to a beautiful former Ziegfeld Follies chorus line dancer, with whom he had four daughters and one son, and he stuck to a small but tightly connected social group primarily composed of himself, Al Miller, Philip Dameo, Michael Leon, Abe Green, Sam Klein, and Moe Dalitz.

Catena excelled at golf and played often, either at Crestmont with my father and Longie Zwillman or at Boca Rio Country Club with Jack Parker, a well-known New York developer I also represented in the 1970s.

"Your father was a hell of a golfer," Catena once told me. "He never let me win—not even once."

"And you let him walk away from that?" I asked. I was only *half*-joking.

Catena smirked. "Golf's different. That's where we go to relax, to leave the business behind."

I guess it was comforting to know that my father wasn't on Jerry's hit list for his *killer* golf game.

• • •

As the boss of the New Jersey faction of the Genovese family, Catena was the subject of round-the-clock sur- veillance from the FBI and local authorities. As such, they routinely became aware of different plots and moves other mobsters were making against Catena.

One such warning came in April 1963, when the FBI issued an alert that Catena and an asso- ciate of Mike Coppola, who had an interest in the Fontainebleau Hotel in Miami, were the targets of a "shakedown kidnapping"—a favorite way of extorting money from mobsters.

The bulletin from the FBI noted that a confi- dential informant had advised them of the plan and identified mobsters from Chicago and Pennsylvania who were behind the kidnapping plot. The source was

concerned for his own safety and planned to contact
Catena and the other target to warn them.

United States Department of Justice
Federal Bureau of Investigation

Miami, Florida
April 23, 1963

Re: [Redacted]

Information has been received that
[redacted] is contemplating at least two
"shakedown" kidnapings [*sic*] involving
Gerardo V. "Jerry" Catena, one of the
leading racketeering figures from Newark,
New Jersey, and [redacted] also known as
[redacted] Miami racketeering figure who
is an associate of Mike Coppola.

These kidnappings are to take place in
the Miami, Florida area, with Catena being
kidnaped [*sic*] on the occasion of one of
his visits to South Florida. [Redacted]
would be kidnaped [*sic*] while in Miami,
inasmuch as he is associated with the
Fontainebleau Hotel, Miami Beach, and
reportedly looks after Mike Coppola's
interest at that hotel. The individuals
kidnaped [*sic*] will allegedly be held on
board a boat until the arrangements are
made for [redacted] and his associates to
collect the demanded money.

Others reportedly approached by [redacted] to participate in this activity are [redacted], also known as [redacted] who is the reported gunman of the Mannarino group in New Kensington and Pittsburgh, Pennsylvania, as well as [redacted] of Chicago, who is known to have participated in an armed robbery set-up by [redacted] in the Miami area.

Information has further been received to the effect both Catena and [redacted] are being advised of this contemplated action taken against them.

Property of the FBI – This memorandum is loaned to you by the FBI and neither it nor its contents are to be distributed outside the agency to which loaned.

Several months after the plot came to light, the FBI informed Catena of the plan. An FBI memo stated, "Catena was advised and 'he was visibly shaken and requested his wife not be advised of same.'"

Urgent 2-6-64
To Director and Newark
From Miami 061704

Gerardo Catena, AKA, AR.

Catena, Newark commission member, presently residing Intercoastal Apartments, Boca Raton, continues to play golf and visited Hialeah Race Track February 4 last. Track officials were waiting for Catena when he departed from track to advise him not to return. Catena, however, left by unexpected exit, but will be ejected on next return.

Catena advised February 5 last his daughter and husband are arriving this week end and will be staying at the Boca Raton Club for one week. He intends to return to Newark with them, with his wife remaining at the apartment, Boca Raton. He will return in one week, spend two more weeks at Boca Raton, and then return with his wife to the Newark area. He states he is vacationing and involved in no activities in this area.

Catena was advised of the previous information received concerning his possibly being held in the Miami area for ransom. He was visibly shaken and requested his wife not be advised of the same.

Investigation continuing.

Received: 2:21 PM HL

CHAPTER 10

Nobody's Immune:
Jerry Catena, Immunity,
and the Fifth Amendment

In the midsixties, my client Jerry Catena was called to appear before a grand jury investigating the Friars Club of Beverly Hills. The Friars Club had become a hangout for Hollywood celebrities such as George Raft, Clark Gable, the Marx Brothers, Tony Martin, Jerry Lewis, and Dean Martin. These movie stars unwittingly and famously became victims of rampant cheating at high-stakes celebrity poker games—facilitated by numerous peepholes the contractor had hidden throughout the Friars Club building.

"Can you believe it?" Catena said, shaking his head as we reviewed the latest developments. "Hollywood's finest getting played by peepholes and mirrors."

"Nobody's immune," I replied.

I didn't know it at the time, but that word—*immune* (or *immunity*)—would soon become *the* defining issue of my work with Jerry.

I traveled with Jerry to California for this grand jury appearance, anticipating that limited immunity might be granted to require his testimony. Concerned that he would be arrested and confined in California indefinitely, we rented a suite at the Beverly Hills Hotel the Sunday before the grand jury convened. If the worst happened, he'd at least be able to spend a few nights in luxury before being thrown in jail.

As we settled into the suite, Catena looked out at the view of Los Angeles. "You think they'll pin anything on me?" he asked.

"I've spoken with the assistant US attorney," I said. "He assures me it'll be just a few limited questions—nothing that'll require you to get immunity."

"But if they push?" Catena pressed me, his eyes sharp.

"If they push, we walk," I said firmly.

I accompanied Catena to the federal courthouse on the morning of the hearing. The assistant US attorney assured me he would ask only a few limited questions and that he wouldn't delve into criminal matters that might necessitate an immunity agreement. However, this carried significant risks for us: If Catena testified voluntarily, he could inadvertently waive his Fifth Amendment privilege, which could lead to contempt of court charges and possible incarceration if he later refused to testify after being granted immunity.

Catena and I discussed the potential consequences. He decided to testify despite the risks, even if it meant facing contempt charges. He was sworn in, and the prosecutor, as promised, kept his questions short and to the point. Jerry answered ten questions, and we were back at the hotel within the hour.

The relief was palpable. We had successfully navigated the situation without falling into the traps of contempt or self-incrimination.

Upon returning to our suite, we found the door unlocked and a gentleman sitting in the living room. Catena immediately recognized him.

"Moe," he said with a mix of surprise and amusement.

Moe Dalitz, a Cleveland mobster and owner of the Stardust Casino and Hotel in Las Vegas and the La Costa Hotel and Spa in La Costa, California, stood up, grinning. "Jerry," he said, "I thought for sure you'd be cooling your heels in a cell by now."

"Not this time," Catena replied with a smirk.

Dalitz chuckled, "Well, just in case, I had a yacht ready for you down in Mexico. Outfitted for months. You'd have been sipping margaritas while the feds chased their tails."

"Appreciate the thought," Catena said, shaking his head. "But I'm not running."

Realizing the escape plan was unnecessary, Dalitz invited us and our wives to stay at La Costa. We drove down that day and played golf the next morning with actor Kirk Douglas and Sam Klein, one of Catena's few close friends.

Klein was a prominent businessman and president of Bally Vending Company, which manufactured a variety of vending and gambling machines. He was later subpoenaed by the Nevada State Licensing Gambling Commission for consorting with suspected organized crime figures, including Dalitz and his good friend Jerry Catena. This forced Klein to resign from Bally and sell all his stock—though he and his close friends profited substantially from the divestment.

• • •

A few years later, the issue of immunity was at the heart of what would become the single most complicated and drawn-out case of my career.

The New Jersey State Commission of Investigation (SCI) was established in 1969 to investigate organized crime, corruption, and fraud in the state. They held their first hearings in 1970, and unsurprisingly, Catena was summoned to testify.

The SCI initially conducted their hearings in secret, granting witnesses immunity to help prevent them from asserting their Fifth Amendment right to keep their mouths shut. They knew that in order to find out what was *really* going on in New Jersey, they'd have to hand out a stack of "free passes." Otherwise, no one would talk.

Several mob members took the immunity deal and testified.

Later, however, the state decided the SCI hearings needed to be done in public. So they made the shocking move of retroactively releasing the testimony transcripts of everyone who had already testified. That meant all the mobsters who *thought* they were spilling the beans in secret were suddenly exposed.

It was a bad look.

Catena and I discussed it one night at the Gold Room, an exclusive section of the Knoll Golf Club that was reserved for VIP members only. The Gold Room was a place where powerful alliances were formed and critical decisions were made that influenced both legitimate businesses and organized crime operations.

"This immunity business," Catena said in a hushed tone, "it's a double-edged sword."

He leaned back in his chair and took a sip of his drink.

I nodded. "It's meant to protect you, but it can also backfire. If you testify, you could waive your Fifth Amendment rights. That could lead to trouble if they dig too deep."

Catena's eyes narrowed. "And if I don't testify, they can hold me in contempt."

He groaned.

This was a hard position to be in, especially since the mob community—and the exclusive Gold Room in particular—had already been shaken up by SCI revelations.

The SCI's investigation into municipal corruption in Union County had overlapped with ongoing investigations of organized crime figures, which led to a subpoena for Angelo Cali, a major real estate developer and a fellow member of the Gold Room. Cali, a friend of Catena's, testified privately before the SCI and was granted immunity.

He was one of many informants who were later exposed when the SCI made prior testimonies public. Once word got out that Cali had talked, the other Gold Room members severed ties with him.

"Cali . . ." Catena sighed, shaking his head at the thought of his now-exiled friend.

"Cali should've kept his mouth shut," he muttered. "Now look at him—an outcast."

"He made his choice," I said carefully. "But you're not Cali. You won't make that mistake."

Catena decided not to testify. No immunity. No deals. No testimony. Period. He'd rather get locked up for contempt than risk ratting out his friends and associates.

He was found in contempt of court and promptly imprisoned. This was standard operating procedure for the court in this kind of situation. The thinking was that a short stay in a prison cell would *encourage* someone to change their mind. It was more about coercion than punishment.

I visited him in prison shortly after. "You holding up?" I asked.

Catena leaned over, his face calm but resolute. "I'm not talking. Not now, not ever."

"I figured as much," I said. "I've filed a writ of habeas corpus in the US District Court to get you out. It's a long shot, but we'll fight this all the way."

That application was denied, and the Third Circuit Court of Appeals affirmed the denial, keeping Catena behind bars. Because the SCI's power had not yet been constitutionally challenged, I believed we had a good chance of having the US Supreme Court hear the matter and make legal history.

To add star power to the case, I enlisted Edward Bennett Williams, the famed Washington, DC, attorney. The US Supreme Court did indeed grant our petition, and Williams and I argued before the Supreme Court for Catena's release. Unfortunately, in 1972, the Court affirmed the SCI's power to compel testimony and the constitutionality of contempt penalties for those who refused.

Back in the holding cell after the ruling, Catena looked at me with a rare hint of frustration.

"So, that's it? They get to keep me locked up forever?"

"Not forever," I replied, determined. "We'll find another way."

Undeterred by our loss at the Supreme Court, I filed a new action in a New Jersey state court in December 1973, arguing that the contempt order for

Catena's refusal to testify no longer had any coercive impact (that is, it was clear he would *never* testify, no matter how long they kept him behind bars). As such, we argued his indefinite incarceration constituted cruel and unusual punishment. This was the first time such an argument had come before the New Jersey courts.

The trial court agreed with my position, ruling that continued confinement no longer served a coercive purpose and ordering Catena's release.

When I visited Catena to give him the news, he didn't show much emotion, but there was a glint in his eyes. "About time," he said. "I was beginning to think they'd forgotten me in here."

"Not a chance," I assured him. "But it's not over yet. The appellate division stayed the order, and the New Jersey Supreme Court is taking it up next."

The New Jersey Supreme Court accepted the prosecution's appeal, remanding the case and ordering a new trial to determine whether the initial sentence had indeed lost its coercive impact. This development marked a significant moment in our legal battle, as the courts began to consider the humanitarian aspect of long-term imprisonment for contempt, setting the stage for a potentially groundbreaking decision.

In a highly unusual ruling, the court allowed the testimony of Catena's attorneys as evidence in this second trial. Edward Bennett Williams and I testified in open court, asserting that further incarceration would not compel Catena to testify. Catena's wife and daughter also submitted affidavits. The trial court again found that Catena's continued confinement for five years no longer had any coercive effect and ordered his release. However, once again, the appellate division stayed this order, which caused us to take the case to the New Jersey Supreme Court.

In yet another highly unusual ruling, the high court allowed the attorneys to testify on behalf of Catena without waiving the attorney-client privilege. Following our testimony, the court ruled that Catena should be released after five years, and he was finally set free at the age of seventy-five.

In its opinion, the court stated it did not matter that Catena was "adhering to organized crime's oath of silence." The key question was whether "there [was] a substantial likelihood that continued confinement [would] cause Catena to change his mind and testify."

Additionally, the New Jersey Supreme Court succinctly stated, "The great strength of the rule of law in a democratic society is that it applies equally to all persons, the bad as well as the good." The long siege was over.

I picked Catena up from prison. We had a wonderful lunch on the way home, and then we stopped at a local tailor shop, where he bought some new clothes for returning to life as a free man.

As we were leaving, Catena handed me a tie. "A small token," he said. "For getting me out."

. . .

After his release from prison at age seventy-five, Jerry retired to Florida, where he lived a quiet life until he died at the age of ninety-eight.

Representing Jerry Catena for forty years was the height of my long career.

On a personal level, Jerry was the ideal client. He was incredibly brilliant, highly analytical, and open to my advice on every occasion. We would have very focused discussions on all the issues before us, and then he would make firm decisions and not look back or second-guess my advice. On many occasions, he knew a wrong choice could result in his incarceration. Other times, he knew one bad move could cost him his life at the hands of his many rivals. Through it all, he was steadfast in his decision-making and always appreciative of my role as his attorney.

On a professional level, representing Catena put me on the front lines of the debates around Fifth Amendment protections and the fascinating legal area of immunity from prosecution. I had always been keenly interested in the constitutional ramifications of self-incrimination and immunity, and these legal issues were at the core of what I did for Jerry.

When he was called before the New Jersey State Crime Commission and refused to answer questions, we challenged the constitutionality of that body's power to hold him in contempt and incarcerate him. For the first and only time in my career, I had the professional thrill of taking this issue to the United States Supreme Court—an experience every trial attorney dreams of.

Obviously, Jerry Catena did some bad things. I'm not blind to who and what he was. But at the same time, I will always be grateful to him for hiring me and giving me four decades of experiences I never could have had representing anyone else.

CHAPTER 11

Meyer Lansky and the Two Tonys

In the sixties, the lines between organized crime and show business were blurry, to say the least. Entertainers such as Frank Sinatra, Wayne Newton, Marlon Brando, and even Marilyn Monroe have long been suspected of having ties to the mob. Whether these specific stars did or didn't . . . well, let's just say that's a discussion for another day.

But in general, it was common to see business get done in secluded booths of nightclubs or in a performer's dressing room. I personally witnessed my fair share of backroom deals and personal favors between mobsters and entertainers.

One of those encounters has always stood out in my mind—not because it was so extraordinary but rather because it all seemed so . . . *normal*, just one guy doing a personal favor for a buddy. Only this time, the *guy* was a notorious mob boss and the *buddy* was a national icon. And I just stood back and watched it play out.

It was the summer of 1968, and I was in Miami with Tony Pro attending a Teamsters convention. We needed a little break from the mixers and meetups of the convention, so Tony and I took a short walk down Collins Avenue.

We were chatting and taking in the sights when he stopped, pointed at a man across the street, and shouted, "Hey! Hey, Bennett!"

I squinted in the Florida sun and tried to focus on the guy with the big smile who was now walking toward us. When his face became clear to me, I couldn't believe my luck. It was the one and only Tony Bennett, and I was a big fan. I assumed he was in town to perform at some convention function. That was one of the perks of running in the circles I did.

"Tony Pro! It's great to see you," Tony Bennett exclaimed, extending his hand.

"Likewise, Tony," Pro replied. "What brings you to Miami? Work or play?"

"A bit of both," Bennett said with a smile. "I'm here as a guest, maybe to sing a bit."

"Well, we're honored to have you," Pro replied. "I'm surprised you could make time for our little convention."

Tony Bennett's smile faded a bit as he said, "Honestly, I've been having trouble getting booked lately. Things have been pretty slow."

Tony Pro raised an eyebrow. "Really? I thought you were always in demand."

Bennett sighed. "Not as much as I used to be. I'm getting a little worried about what's next."

Before Tony Pro could respond, I noticed a familiar figure in the distance walking his dog. Meyer Lansky, the "financial wizard" of the Jewish mob, had been staying next door at the Americana Hotel. As he approached, it was clear that all three men knew one another well.

Lansky greeted us with a nod. "Tony, Tony," he said, acknowledging both men, then looked at me. "And you must be a friend of Pro's."

Tony Pro quickly made the introductions. "Meyer, this is a good friend of mine, Chris Franzblau. He's been helping me out with some things. And you probably know Tony Bennett."

Lansky smiled faintly. "Of course. Who doesn't know Tony Bennett?"

Bennett chuckled, though this time I sensed a little uneasiness. "Good to see you, Meyer. We were just talking about a little trouble I've been having getting booked."

Lansky tilted his head. "Trouble? A man with your talent?"

Bennett nodded. "It's the way the business goes sometimes."

Tony Pro stepped in. "I was thinking about trying to help Bennett get a gig at the Sands. You know, shake things up a bit."

Lansky considered this for a moment. "The Sands, huh? Well, that's a good place to get back in the game. Pro, you still have those connections there?"

Tony Pro smirked. "Sure I do. The Sands and I go way back. Labor issues, union matters—I've handled plenty of that out there. I'll see what I can do, Tony."

Bennett's face lit up with hope. "I'd really appreciate that. A break like that could make all the difference."

"We'll make it happen," Tony Pro said confidently.

Months later, I found myself back at the Sands Hotel, and who was performing in the cocktail lounge next to the casino? None other than Tony Bennett.

Watching him onstage, I thought back to that chance encounter in Miami. I asked around and learned that Bennett had been performing there regularly for the past several weeks.

It wasn't long before his career took off again.

Whenever people ask me about how dark and dirty and gritty mob dealings must be, my mind always goes back to that beautiful day in the Miami sunshine, when I watched two mobsters lift the spirits of an entertainment icon. I have no idea if Tony Bennett ever had to *repay* that favor in some way or if there was some unspoken leverage that was gained in that chance encounter.

Probably.

But what I do know is that I got to enjoy Tony Bennett's music career well into the nineties and beyond—and that might not have happened if the two Tonys hadn't bumped into each other that fateful day in Florida.

• • •

My trip to Miami with Tony Pro for the Teamsters convention was the first time I met Meyer Lansky, but it certainly would not be the last. I ran into him several more times over the next few years and eventually represented him in an interesting trial at the end of his mob career.

One of those chance meetings with Lansky happened at the Sands Hotel and Casino in Las Vegas, a hub of activity for entertainers and mobsters alike. Vegas had something to offer everybody.

On one trip, I was in Las Vegas representing Charles Turner, a pit boss at the Sands Casino. The Department of Justice was conducting a major criminal investigation of money laundering and tax evasion at the hotel. A key player in the investigation was Doc Stacher, executive director at the Sands who had a family connection to my longtime associate Abner "Longie" Zwillman. My client, Turner, was under the microscope alongside Stacher, who was represented by the well-known lawyer Ed Williams.

As I was strolling through the lobby of the Sands, I spotted Meyer Lansky sitting in the lounge. He noticed me and gestured for me to join him.

"Busy night?" I asked, sliding into the chair opposite him.

"Always is," Lansky replied, his voice calm. "How's your client holding up?"

"Stacher's a tough one," I said. "But we've got Ed Williams on the case. If anyone can get him out of this mess, it's Ed."

Lansky nodded. "Williams knows his way around a courtroom. And he's got the connections."

"He does," I agreed. "But this case is different. The DOJ is coming down hard. They want to make an example out of Stacher."

Lansky leaned back, considering this. "They always want to make an example out of someone. It's just a matter of how far they're willing to go."

"They're pushing for deportation," I said. "Stacher's not a US citizen, so they're using that as leverage."

Lansky's expression didn't change. "And if he's deported?"

"He'll be gone for good," I said. "He'll have to put up a $250,000 bond and agree to never return."

Lansky took a sip of his drink. "And where does that leave you?"

"I'm still representing Turner," I said. "But Stacher's case is a warning shot. They're coming after everyone."

Lansky's eyes narrowed slightly. "Even me?"

"Could be," I admitted. "They're not just after the little fish this time. They're going for the big ones too."

We parted ways that night, and Ed Williams and I went on to successfully defend Stacher and Turner, who were free to go. Stacher was not deported.

Neither of us knew it at the time, but that friendly conversation over drinks at the Sands planted a seed that would bear fruit for both me and Lansky years later. He had moved to Israel in 1970 to avoid prosecution on federal tax evasion charges, but the United States was trying hard to extradite him to Miami. Morris Shelisky, a high-powered New York criminal attorney who had worked with Ed Williams and me on the Stacher case, knew Lansky and recommended me for his extradition case.

When Shelisky approached me about representing Lansky, he hoped I could land the same outcome for Lansky that we had for Stacher. Only this time, the goal was to keep my client *out* of the United States, not to keep him *in* it.

Our legal strategy was to prove that Lansky didn't pose a clear and present danger to the welfare of Israel by living there. Despite our argument, Israel yielded to the demands of the Department of Justice, and Israel's highest court ruled in 1972 that Lansky was not entitled to Israeli citizenship despite being Jewish.

Lansky then sued for permission to remain in the country under the Law of Return, which grants every Jew the intrinsic right to enter Israel as an immigrant. This also failed.

The court's decision was a major blow to Lansky. Despite his efforts to remain in Israel, including claims of his retirement and contributions to Jewish causes, the Israeli high court's decision highlighted the severity of his criminal background.

His reputation, it seemed, had caught up with him.

When I met with Lansky after the ruling, he was surprisingly calm. "They're sending me back," he said simply.

"I'm sorry, Meyer," I said. "We did everything we could."

Lansky shrugged. "It was always a long shot. But I appreciate the effort."

"We're not done yet," I tried to reassure him. "There's more to do in the US courts."

Lansky smiled faintly. "That's what I hear. But sometimes, the fight is over."

In the end, Lansky was extradited to Florida, where he stood trial and was convicted of contempt of a grand jury—but acquitted of tax evasion—in 1973. Other charges were dropped in 1974. He lived out his final years in Florida, passing away from lung cancer in 1983 at the age of eighty.

CHAPTER 12

"Sam the Plumber" DeCavalcante and the Infamous FBI Wiretaps

The 1960s was an interesting time to be representing active members of the mob. The FBI was getting more and more involved in organized crime investigations, and they had jumped headfirst into the burgeoning field of wiretaps and other forms of electronic surveillance. Being a good attorney meant learning how to navigate surprising recordings and lengthy transcripts of my clients in what they assumed to be private conversations with their "associates."

This was especially true for me in the case of mobster Simone DeCavalcante, better known as Sam the Plumber. He was indicted for conspiracy to commit extortion, loan-sharking, illicit gambling, and labor kickbacks in 1968, and this case came with a mountain of surprises from the FBI and Department of Justice.

It was one of the most challenging cases—and biggest messes—of my career.

DeCavalcante was deeply involved in the world of organized crime. He was a tall, handsome, soft-spoken man who was always impeccably dressed, as if he had stepped right out of a Saks Fifth Avenue window display. Under the watchful eye of his uncle and crime boss Nick Delmore of Long Branch, New Jersey, DeCavalcante thrived in various mob enterprises, specializing in loan-sharking and gambling.

Nick Delmore had led "the family" for many years. He had gotten his start running illegal whiskey operations during the Prohibition era of the 1930s. In the early sixties, Delmore retired to a golfing community in Neptune, New Jersey, turning his authority in the criminal organization over to his nephew, DeCavalcante. This made Sam the Plumber *the* boss of New Jersey. Even the New York Mafia acknowledged DeCavalcante's authority over Jersey. When it came to New Jersey, he *was* the mob.

DeCavalcante partnered with Lawrence Wolfson, a former felon, and they conducted their operations out of the posh offices of Sam's plumbing supply warehouse—hence his infamous nickname.

Those offices had a constant flow of people coming and going, each discussing some kind of illicit business with Sam. There were low-level thugs, high-level capos, enforcers, "respectable" business owners, politicians, civic leaders, and members of law enforcement. Practically anyone who did business with the Jersey mob spent some time in DeCavalcante's plumbing supply office.

So when the FBI planted listening devices throughout the offices in 1965, they secured a gold mine of evidence against not only Sam DeCavalcante but against practically everyone he did business with.

Those "bugs" caught everything that happened in the office, both criminal activities and personal encounters. They even captured evidence of sexual encounters between DeCavalcante and his partner's sister, an attractive woman who served as their bookkeeper.

DeCavalcante was ultimately indicted, and he hired me to defend him. Neither of us knew at that time about the thousands and thousands of pages of transcripts the FBI had of his operations.

When defending a criminal case, it's standard practice to send the government a bill of particulars, which is essentially a set of interrogatories. This document typically asks formal questions, such as whether there was any electronic surveillance and requests for details such as times, dates, and other pertinent information.

"Mr. DeCavalcante," I explained, "we need to be prepared for a long legal battle. I've submitted the bill of particulars, but I anticipate delays. It's standard procedure, and sometimes the government takes its time responding."

DeCavalcante nodded, his expression inscrutable. "I understand. Just keep me updated. The last thing I want is to be caught off guard."

Getting "caught off guard" would turn out to be a massive understatement for what was going to happen to us.

The government normally responds to the bill of particulars within a reasonable time frame, but there's rarely a rush to go to trial in criminal cases. That's fine with me. Delays can work in your favor, as witnesses forget details over time, pass away, or move out of the area. So I wasn't particularly concerned when the answers to the bill of particulars and other document demands didn't arrive promptly.

The case appeared on the court calendar several times over the next year and a half. Each time, I pointed out that we hadn't received the necessary discovery materials, and the judge would push the trial date back. Having previously worked in the US Attorney's Office, I knew the people there and wasn't in any hurry to push for the answers. I was content to wait as long as the prosecutors wanted to delay the trial.

But suddenly, in 1968, all hell broke loose.

US Attorney David Satz retired, and Robert Horowitz was tapped to temporarily fill the position. Soon after Horowitz got up and running, the attorney general lit a fire under him to get the infamous "Sam the Plumber Case" up and running. Whether it was from haste or simply to catch us off guard (probably the latter), Horowitz filed his response to the bill of particulars and included five huge volumes of wiretap transcripts with the court—without giving me, the defense counsel, any notice.

But they still hadn't informed me.

I was sitting in my office completely unaware of what was happening when my phone rang. A reporter (not an agent of the court, but a newspaper reporter) said that the government had finally filed the answers to the bill of particulars—by filing several thousand pages of FBI transcripts, including electronic surveillance tapes from DeCavalcante's office in Kenilworth.

"What's this about?" I asked the reporter, trying to mask my alarm.

"You haven't heard?" the reporter said. "The government just released a mountain of tapes of your client and his business dealings. I'm calling for a statement."

It had been dead silent for eighteen months, and then the prosecution abruptly dropped transcripts and recordings of literally thousands of conversations between my client and his associates that were captured over a monthslong wiretapping operation. Making matters worse, they held a press conference *as they filed the papers with the court*. The general public knew about all this new evidence before I did.

It was the first I or DeCavalcante had ever heard of the FBI recordings. It was damning evidence, and I was caught completely flat-footed. It was infuriating—and it was big news. It dominated headlines all that week.

The tapes were packed with details of the lifetime activities, unlawful conduct, and personal relationships of individuals from all walks of life, many of whom were highly embarrassed by the revelations. The recordings exposed the activities of organized crime targets and their connections with highly respected businessmen, revealing their conspiratorial conduct as they sought the aid of none other than Sam the Plumber.

The release of these surveillance tapes was a pivotal moment in my career. And it was obvious once I read the transcripts why the government had initially withheld them. They exposed what was really going on behind closed doors in the DeCavalcante crime family, bringing to light the cunning and often brutal tactics used to maintain control over the mob's activities in New Jersey.

Perhaps most importantly, these tapes provided irrefutable evidence that there was, in fact, a well-organized criminal organization led by crime families with highly defined hierarchies. This had often been speculated but had been long denied by authorities and the press. It was what we'd call today a conspiracy theory. But this one was proved true, and no one could deny it any longer.

The report on one transcript read:

On 6/10/65, NK-2461-C* reported that during a meeting between SAMULE RIZZO DE CAVALANTE and MICHAEL PUGLIA, the latter said that he had been advised by JOE LA SELVA on Friday night (6/4/65). PUGLIA said he told LA SELVA that due to a prior commitment, it would be impossible for him to attend and he asked LA

SELVA to explain this to DE CAVALCANTE when they met. He said he told LA SELVA that he would visit DE CAVALCANTE during the following week.

From PUGLIA's remarks, it would appear that LA SELVA was present at the Sunday meeting which was DE CAVALCANTE, himself, said the purpose of this meeting was to announce to the hierarchy of the family that JOSEPH SFERRA had been removed as Caporegnia and that PAUL FAINA had been appointed in his stead.

This was just one of many conversations and reports that proved the existence of an *organized* criminal family and enterprise operating in New Jersey with a formal, businesslike structure.

In a recording from June 1965, DeCavalcante was asked by two other mob members to mediate a dispute between them. He explained that members of another family would be treated as *Amico Nostro*, a term meaning a friend of the Cosa Nostra (the Sicilian Mafia), as a courtesy—emphasizing that "our thing is our thing." With this approach, DeCavalcante successfully settled the dispute, and it was implied that a "disappearance" of sorts would be arranged.

"Sam, we need your help," one connected labor leader in the construction industry said on the tape. "There's a problem with the other family. We need to settle this before it escalates."

DeCavalcante responded smoothly, "I'll handle it. Let's keep this under control and make sure everyone walks away satisfied."

The conversation then shifted to an interview of sorts for hiring perpetrators from another organized crime family based in a distant area. After the dispute was resolved, an unidentified person referred to as Tony recounted a murder he had committed years earlier.

"We kidnapped this guy, Fillipo," Tony said. "Put him in a car and drove him to a farm. We cut his throat and buried him."

Tony noted that when they later dug up the body to move it, he was shocked by what he saw. "We dug him up after he died, and his hair was still growing. The dead man was hairy—never saw this before."*

One of the criminal activities revealed in these tapes was the payments made to the mob by many of New Jersey's most prominent builders. The tapes

---

* FBI transcript, 1965, p. 1465.

contained multiple discussions with Joe Wilf, a leading builder and patriarch of the Wilf family—one of the wealthiest families in the country, now owners of the Minnesota Vikings. The transcripts confirm ongoing negotiations between Wilf and another major developer, Sam Halpern, regarding the amount of payoffs to the union to ensure the use of nonunion labor.

```
United States Government
Memorandum

To: SAC, Newark (92-722)
Date: 7/6/65
From: Clerk William P. Nugent
Subject: Samuel Rizzo de Cavalcante,
aka AR

    NK 2461-C* advised De Cavalcante and
Larry Wolfson met with Sam Halpern and
Joe Wilf on 6/23/65. Wilf and Halpern are
building contractors in the Union County,
N.J., area./ De Cavalcante complained to
Wilf and Halpern about their inability to
supply him with union payoff money after
De Cavalcante has negotiated with various
union representatives for labor peace (on
their building projects) for payoffs. De
Cavalcante pointed out that he had paid
out $5700-$5800 to union representatives,
who have their local's [sic] not working on
Wilf and Halpern's Oak Tree Road project
```

in Edison, N.J. Halpern promised De Cavalcante that they would repay him $6,000 as soon as they receive the mortgage money on this job. Wolfson asked Wilf and Halpern to pay Kenworth Corporation for the work Kenworth did at this project and Halpern promised Kenworth would also be paid out of this mortgage money.

NK 2461-C* learned Kenworth has not received any money for completed work from Halpern and Wilf on two or three jobs in Plainfield, N.J., and one job in Parsippany, N.J.

NK 2461-C* said De Cavalcante explained to Wilf and Halpern that when he fixes a union representative, they expect to be paid immediately and not have to wait till a job is completed. De Cavalcante told Wilf that he never billed them for incidental expenses (e.g. gifts, wining and dining) he incurred by developing these union representatives to the point where they will accept the payoff Wilf and Halpern can pay and not the larger amount of payoff these union representatives usually ask for. De Cavalcante pointed out that on one of the Plainfield, N.J., jobs he had to sit down with twelve union representatives and threatened all twelve with the result that they took the picket line they had off this Plainfield job. De Cavalcante pointed out any one of these twelve men could make trouble for him in revenge for his forcing this picket line off this job.

NK 2461-C* advised De Cavalcante told Wilf and Halpern that they owe De Cavalcante money for his services and for services of the late Nick Delmore dating back to the time when Delmore became sick and subsequently died.

NK 2461-C* related De Cavalcante told Wilf and Halpern that certain union representatives and their New York "sponsors" are pressing De Cavalcante for money on the 3,000 apartment units they and Joe Kuschner (ph) are currently building. Wolfson said a (FNU?) Bradley (ph) from New York has been giving De Cavalcante a bad time of late (illegible) on some part of Wilf and Halpern's building (illegible) De Cavalcante pointed out that the (illegible) do not bother him as they have no (illegible) New Jersey.

NK 2461-C* said De Cavalcante and Wolfson complained? That they take all the risks in setting up these payoff deals with union representatives. Wolfson claimed he would be ruined if ever he was involved in any investigation of these payoffs or was brought to court and found guilty of practicing "graft negotiations". De Cavalcante pointed out that these union representatives usually contact him telephonically in his office and De Cavalcante has no assurance that the phone they are calling on or the phone he is using is not tapped.

NK 2461-C* said Wolfson told Halpern and Wilf that he was at a wake in Brooklyn, N.Y. the previous week and one of the union representatives involved in their Parsippany apartment project told Wolfson that Halpern and Wilf will have to pay $100 a unit for labor peace. NK 2461-C* learned Wilf and Halpern use a certain percentage of non-union labor on their construction projects and prefer to use mostly non-union labor which is cheaper and for which they have to pay union representatives money to overlook this situation.

NK 2461-C* advised De Cavalcante rejoined them and Halpern complained of having trouble with the mason's union local representative, one Tommy Lo Petro (ph), on their North Plainfield, N.J., job. Halpern also complained that he paid off the painter's union local's [sic] representative on this job and learned De Cavalcante also paid him. De Cavalcante admitted he paid him so this man was doubly paid. De Cavalcante was angered at this man accepting a double payoff but told Halpern not to say anything to this man as it would be bad for Halpern to embarrass this man.

NK 2461-C* advised Wolfson reminded Wilf and Halpern that Kenworth had only received payment checks for the Bayberry (ph) job and nothing for the work completed on the Parsippany job.

NK 2461-C* related De Cavalcante told Halpern and Wilf that in the future he will make union representatives payoffs in three parts. A third before the job commences; another third before the job is almost half completed; and the final third before the job is completed De Cavalcante said he will not pay any part before receiving the money aforehand and if Wilf and Halpern do not like this arrangement. Then they should forget they know him.

NK 2461-C* advised De Cavalcante told Wilf that all the unions [sic] representatives on any particular job have to be paid off. If one is only paid off, then the others in jealousy will strike the job and cause much union trouble at the job.

NK 2461-C* said Halpern told De Cavalcante that Wilf and he are going to give De Cavalcante $5,000 cash for payoffs on the 174 garden apartment units on one of the Plainfield, N.J., jobs. De Cavalcante refused this $10,000 as the deal he made with the union representatives on this job calls for $100 a unit or $17,400. Halpern said this job was 50-60 per cent [sic] union and De Cavalcante should not have agreed to $17,400. De Cavalcante told

Halpern that he did not tell him that Halpern was going to use 50-60 per cent [sic] union so the deal De Cavalcante made will have to be honored even if De Cavalcante has to pay $17,400 or any part of it out of his own pocket. De Cavalcante again told Halpern not to see him in the future if this happens. Halpern and Wilf reluctantly agreed to give De Cavalcante $10,000 within the next two weeks and $8,000 over the next two months to make up the necessary $17,400. De Cavalcante said in the future they should keep him advised of the percentage of union labor they have to utilize on any particular job.

NK 2461-C* said De Cavalcante indicated to Wilf and Halpern that they and Joe Kuschner (?) (ph) may have to pay high to use non-union labor on the projects they are building, including those in the Parsippany – Denville, N.J. area. De Cavalcante said the union representatives want close to $200,000 in payoff money for this building Kuschner, Halpern, and Wilf are or will be doing. NK 2461-C* learned Kuschner and De Cavalcante have already been together and made an agreement on the payoff money for these projects Kuschner has under way. Kuschner has already sent some part of this payoff money to De Cavalcante and Wolfson.

NK 2461-C* learned Halpern had made the payoff deal on the Bayberry Garden job which is completed. This job was 100 per cent [sic] non-union and Halpern made considerable money on the Bayberry job which is in Scotch Plains, N.J.

NK 2461-C* said De Cavalcante commented that he had stuck his neck out for Halpern and Wilf on an Edison, N.J., job (Oak Tree Road job?) of theirs. De Cavalcante claimed this job became so hot that the Edison Chief of Police and Police Director were personally observing it. De Cavalcante said strike breakers had been imported into Edison to break the picket line on this job and it would have been a big mess only that De Cavalcante made the deal which settled the trouble on this job.

NK 2461-C* related De Cavalcante told Wilf and Halpern that any payoff deal he makes, he will stand behind it. De Cavalcante told them that he wants payoff money from them in the future as he asks for it and does not expect to be kept waiting. De Cavalcante told them that anytime they feel they can do better with someone else, to arrange their payoffs for the, them they are welcome to stop seeing him.

Another prominent and politically influential family mentioned in the tapes is the Kushner family.

Joseph Kushner (born Joseph Berkowitz) had been born in Poland in the 1920s and immigrated with his wife to the United States after World War II. He settled in New Jersey and worked as a carpenter before starting his own business and building wealth as a real estate investor and developer.

If the name Kushner sounds familiar, it's likely because Joseph's grandson, Jared Kushner, is the son-in-law of US President Donald Trump and played a prominent role in Trump's first administration.

The tapes generated an enormous amount of publicity, given the massive volume of information related to organized crime figures and other well-known names mentioned. Not long after their release, while all sorts of rumors and gossip were swirling around not only organized crime but also on the bigger issue of the FBI's use of secret listening devices, I received a call from the American Civil Liberties Union (ACLU) in Atlanta.

"Is it true the release of these tapes was a diversion?" asked the ACLU representative.

"I can't say for certain," I replied. "But it's clear there's a lot of political maneuvering going on."

They speculated that the government's release of these tapes was an attempt to counteract the negative publicity surrounding other illegal tapes that had surfaced. At the time of the disclosure, the government was already facing public backlash over the illegal surveillance of Dr. Martin Luther King Jr. and Cassius Clay (later known as Muhammad Ali), both iconic figures in the Black community. The racial climate in the country was explosive, with race riots and protests breaking out in several cities, and adverse political consequences were unfolding.

Many have speculated that the government wanted to demonstrate a *positive* use of their new wiretapping capability. The most spectacular example they could come up with, it seems, was to blow the lid off the existence and pervasiveness of organized crime families across New Jersey and other states.

I must admit the whole affair was quite embarrassing for me as DeCavalcante's lawyer. The media was quick to criticize me, and I received a lot of negative press. It was frustrating because, although my legal strategy was sound—that is, not being more active in pressing the government to respond to my bill of particulars—the outcome was disastrous. I never could have anticipated such a flagrant and public surprise from the prosecution.

However, the release of those tapes, while shocking, did not affect DeCavalcante's legal situation in the way the government had hoped. In fact, it had the opposite effect: It led to the dismissal of the indictment at that time. The government would ultimately prevail, though, as other ongoing investigations unrelated to the tapes eventually resulted in further charges against DeCavalcante, leading to his eventual imprisonment.

Ironically, the release of the DeCavalcante recordings had a much more negative affect on the FBI than it did on my client. Up through the midsixties, the Bureau had a sterling reputation, but this massive disclosure, combined with other controversial activities, began to erode the public's trust in the agency. Ever since this scandal, the FBI, once seen as untouchable, has become the subject of critical scrutiny—and the subject of countless conspiracy theories.

While it's become common in many circles to insult and distrust the FBI over the years, I want to point out that, even though I was at the center of this PR disaster, the release of the DeCavalcante tapes did not change my overall respect for the FBI. Having worked with the FBI for a long time during my tenure at the US Attorney's Office, my experience with them was consistently professional. I had always felt a deep respect for the investigations they conducted, and that respect remained unchanged even after this incident.

To me, the integrity of their work was never in question.

As for Sam the Plumber, he served a little over half of his five-year sentence on an unrelated conviction at the federal penitentiary in Atlanta, Georgia. He retired to Florida in 1976, where he tried to drum up support for building a new resort casino, but voters shot it down. He died of natural causes in Fort Lauderdale in 1997 and was brought back home and laid to rest in New Jersey.

CHAPTER 13

It's Not as Glamorous as It Is in the Movies

I've seen a lot of gangster movies, and I've known a lot of gangsters in real life. So you can trust me when I tell you . . . *the movies lie.*

In 2014, director Clint Eastwood released *Jersey Boys*, his film adaptation of the hit Broadway musical of the same name. The musical had been selling out theaters since its opening in 2005, and it went on to become the twelfth longest-running show in Broadway history. It won Tony, Grammy, and Olivier awards throughout its eleven-year run,* though the movie version, as is often the case, has been less well regarded.

I loved the musical, and I thought the movie was fine. But watching the story of Frankie Valli play out onstage and on the big screen really drove home the reality that movies lie. Even films based on real-life events are dramatized, sensationalized, and otherwise *assisted* by made-up elements and shamefully unfaithful portrayals of the actual human beings who inspired the characters on-screen.

In Eastwood's *Jersey Boys*, actor Christopher Walken portrayed the affable and charismatic mob boss Angelo "Gyp" DeCarlo. Audiences couldn't help but like the guy. Problem is, that's not at all who Gyp DeCarlo was in real life. Or at least, that's not *all* he was.

The Gyp DeCarlo I knew was a brutal, ruthless mob boss with an army of enforcers who loved nothing more than taking out their aggression on anyone foolish enough to owe DeCarlo money.

I should know.

I represented one of those fools.

---

* Andrew Gans, "Jersey Boys Ends Record-Breaking Broadway Run Jan. 15," *Playbill*, January 15, 2017, https://playbill.com /article/jersey-boys-ends-record-breaking-broadway-run-jan-15.

Jerry Zelmanowitz, who operated under the alias Jerry Martin, was involved in the textile business run by the Teamsters Union in New York. Originally from Short Hills, New Jersey, Zelmanowitz was a successful businessman, but he developed a serious gambling problem that led him into a bottomless pit of debt. That debt regrettably led him to Gyp DeCarlo's door.

Gyp DeCarlo was a notable figure within the Genovese family, and he was deeply embedded in organized crime. He was revered for his intimidating presence and sharp business acumen. He famously converted a barn into a lavish restaurant and night-club on Route 22 in Springfield, New Jersey, which he used for both business and personal entertainment.

Against his better judgment, Zelmanowitz borrowed money from DeCarlo to pay off his gambling debts. But that just took him out of the frying pan and into the fire. Now it wasn't just bookies Zelmanowitz had to worry about; it was being indebted to one of the mob's craftiest—and roughest—bosses.

When Zelmanowitz inevitably got behind on his payments, DeCarlo *suggested* he take out a loan against his house. And wouldn't you believe it, DeCarlo even helped set Zelmanowitz up with a lender. A few signatures later, and Zelmanowitz had added a second layer of debt—owed to Michael Leon, a known associate of DeCarlo—on top of what he *already owed* Gyp. Zelmanowitz just kept digging himself deeper and deeper into a hole he'd never be able to climb out of.

One afternoon in the midst of all this, Zelmanowitz stopped by DeCarlo's barn to make a payment. When he walked in, he realized he wasn't the only debtor making a payment that day. Louis Saperstein from South Orange, New Jersey, was also there. Saperstein was a successful insurance broker who, like Zelmanowitz, had a big gambling problem. He owed DeCarlo approximately $400,000, and he was also having trouble getting the money to DeCarlo on time. So the mob boss decided to take his payment in blood.

Zelmanowitz watched in horror as DeCarlo's enforcers hung Saperstein on a hook, tasered him, and beat him mercilessly. He quickly realized that the timing of his visit wasn't an accident. DeCarlo clearly wanted Zelmanowitz to see the assault on Saperstein. It wasn't merely a punishment for Saperstein; it was a warning for Zelmanowitz.

The message was clear: *You're next . . . if you don't pay.*

Weeks later, when Saperstein had yet to return with the money, he was shot several times in front of his girlfriend's house in Springfield. He miraculously survived the attack and spilled his guts to the FBI from his hospital bed, begging for their protection in exchange for his testimony against DeCarlo. The plea for his life backfired. DeCarlo got wind of the call, and Saperstein never left the hospital. He *somehow* died from arsenic poisoning while recovering from his gunshot wounds.

What are the chances?

Unbeknownst to both Saperstein and DeCarlo, the FBI was already looking into Gyp's operations. Weeks earlier, they'd obtained search warrants that enabled them to plant listening devices in the barn. They even had the full audio recording of Saperstein's assault the day Zelmanowitz was there!

More than that, the FBI had recordings of many of DeCarlo's business conversations and associates—including other Mafia members, business leaders, and politicians. Among those recorded was Hugh Addonizio, the sitting mayor of Newark and a former congressman in the US House of Representatives. Shockingly, Addonizio had also borrowed substantial sums of money from DeCarlo to cover his gambling debts. The exposure of Addonizio's criminal connections led to his indictment, the end of his political career, and a twelve-year sentence in prison.

Zelmanowitz was summoned to testify against DeCarlo before two grand juries in Newark—one at the Essex County level and the other federal. I represented Zelmanowitz, whom I advised to assert his Fifth Amendment right against self-incrimination and thereby refuse to testify. At least, that's what he did for the Essex County appearance. When it came time for his federal grand jury appearance, Zelmanowitz never showed up. He had vanished without a trace.

DeCarlo went on to face an indictment for conspiracy to murder Saperstein, for which he was convicted and sentenced to twelve years in prison. While incarcerated, his health deteriorated due to cancer. Several of DeCarlo's celebrity associates, including Frank Sinatra, spoke to then-President Nixon on his behalf, and Nixon granted DeCarlo a pardon in 1973. He died shortly after his release.

But what happened to my client, Jerry Zelmanowitz? After he failed to show for his grand jury appearance, I found out that he had contacted the assistant United States attorney without me. They put him in the witness protection program, and I never heard from him again.

That's probably where Zelmanowitz and the feds *wish* his story ended. But it's not.

Zelmanowitz—along with his wife, uncle, and his wife's parents—were given completely new identities and relocated to San Francisco, where he started a children's textile manufacturing business with a partner.

The partnership eventually soured, resulting in litigation between them. His partner hired a private detective who broke into Zelmanowitz's desk drawer and found four Social Security cards bearing the names of the new identities of Zelmanowitz, his wife, and his wife's parents. The detective noticed that the numbers on the cards were in sequential order, which was frankly impossible. It was clear the Social Security cards were fake. Armed with that information, the detective kept poking around and ultimately exposed their true identities as part of the lawsuit proceedings. Zelmanowitz disappeared once again soon after. I don't know if the government hid him again or if he decided to take his chances on his own.

This incident highlighted a broader issue with the federal Witness Security Program, which was created to protect former criminals who agreed to testify against organized crime figures. The program, which provided new identities complete with counterfeit Social Security cards, driver's licenses, and fabricated job histories, was instrumental in securing more than three thousand convictions against mob members. However, it also came under scrutiny for the risks it posed to the unsuspecting public, who may unknowingly interact with these former criminals. Plus, many relocated witnesses reverted to their criminal ways, causing significant harm in their new communities. All these decades later, the program's cost-effectiveness and ethical implications are still subjects of serious debate.

Perhaps the only good thing to come out of all this was DeCarlo's barn-turned-restaurant, the Belmont Tavern. It was reopened by DeCarlo's former right-hand man and chauffeur, who had also worked at the barn as a terrific chef. The establishment remains a fixture in Newark, frequented by a mix of lawyers, judges, businessmen, and gangsters. It's a testament to the era of mob influence in New Jersey.

CHAPTER 14

Senator for Sale

It's a strange thing to be known as a go-to resource in organized crime circles. Most people would probably prefer it if the country's most notorious mobsters did not know who they were or where to find them. Not me. My reputation has kept me in the Rolodexes (and now Contact apps) of some of the most despicable people in the world.

Whenever my phone rang during my prime "mob lawyer" years, I never worried about who was on the other end. Oftentimes, sure, it was a capo or enforcer who needed help. Other times, though, it wasn't a member of a crime family at all. It was just someone who was . . . *connected*.

Such was the time I got a call from Bill Yuan, a successful Chinese businessman in Ridgewood, New Jersey.

William "Bill" Yuan's story was the epitome of the American Dream. He owned a large injection molding manufacturing company called Moldeico, in Edison, New Jersey, and ran a major warehousing operation for imported goods on the Jersey waterfront. Bill was a man of refinement, education, and significant social standing. At the height of his career, he was honored by the White House as Businessman of the Year. He was truly an inspiration—primarily because he built his empire from nothing, starting with empty pockets and big dreams.

Bill's journey began in 1948, when, as a youth, he was on one of the last planes out of China before the country fell to communist forces. Around the time General Chiang Kai-shek was leaving China, Bill and his family relocated to Taiwan. Years later, Bill married his childhood sweetheart and immigrated to the United States, initially leaving their two young sons behind with his parents while he pursued an engineering degree at the University of Kansas. After graduating, Bill brought his family to New Jersey, where he and his wife had two more sons.

Over the years, Bill's intelligence, hard work, and grit led to exponential success, eventually putting him in some pretty influential circles. He managed those connections with the precision of an engineer. Every relationship, every conversation, every detail of every encountered mattered to Bill. He knew *real* business wasn't conducted in board rooms or corporate offices; rather, he worked most of his magic over dinners, drinks, and some friendly wagers.

Bill's patience and craftiness paid off big-time when it came to his relationship with US Senator James "Big Jim" Oliver Eastland, a powerful political player from Mississippi. Eastland, himself an attorney and plantation owner, held significant seniority in the Senate, where he chaired various committees throughout the thirty-five years he held the office. At the senator's invitation, Bill often traveled to Washington, DC, where they dined together and engaged in high-stakes card games.

Bill was a skilled gambler—so much so that the dealers and pit bosses at Las Vegas's Desert Inn both admired and feared his finesse. Nonetheless, Senator Eastland had a knack for beating Bill most of the time, winning substantial sums of Bill's money in the process.

Was the senator an even more gifted card sharp than Bill?

No.

Rather, Bill let him win.

A lot.

The distinguished gentleman from Mississippi was equally "lucky" whenever he and Bill went to the racetrack to enjoy an afternoon of horseracing. Bill placed the bets on their behalf, and he graciously divided his winnings with Eastland. There were *always* winnings, too, because Bill didn't leave anything to chance. He always placed several bets on several different horses in every race.

The senator quickly caught on to the fact that every time he was around Bill for any length of time, he'd go home with money in his pocket. Neither of them ever suggested it was a bribe, and both would be horribly shocked and offended if someone made the charge. How could it be a bribe if the good Senator Eastland won all that money fair and square?

Heaven forbid.

That said, all that winning did indeed tend to ingratiate the senator to Bill. One evening as they played cards after dinner, Senator Eastland leaned back in his chair, sipping his bourbon. "Bill, you're too generous for your own good," he said with a grin, after another winning hand.

Bill chuckled, shuffling the deck. "Just luck of the draw, Senator. But one of these days, maybe *I'll* get lucky too."

Senator Eastland smiled and nodded. His tone shifted, getting a little more serious as he said, "You know, Bill, I've been keeping an eye on something that might interest you: three decommissioned navy cargo ships. They're all still in good shape, and they're gonna go for a steal."

Bill raised an eyebrow. "Ships? Why me?"

The senator leaned in, his voice lowering. "These aren't just any ships. They're surplus, and with a little investment, they could be worth far more than the asking price. Besides, *with the right connections*, you wouldn't have to worry about losing them in a public auction or having the price bid up by another buyer."

Not long after that fruitful conversation, Bill became the partial owner of three large cargo ships from the navy's mothballed fleet off the Pacific coast near San Diego.

Bill and several business associates formed a partnership and arranged to buy the ships. The senator, whose committee oversaw surplus military equipment, had suggested that Bill and his associates offer to purchase the ships for $100,000 each, along with a $300,000 bond as collateral to ensure that the ships wouldn't be scrapped.

Senator Eastland monitored the transaction, ensuring that it bypassed the typical government auction process. After the purchase, Bill's group used the ships as floating warehouses for wheat in Kaohsiung, a seaport near Taiwan. Since the ships lacked functioning engines, they were towed across the Pacific and docked in Kaohsiung Harbor. US government inspectors later visited to ensure the contract terms were being met.

All was well . . . for a while.

Years later, in the late 1960s, the price of steel skyrocketed. Bill and his partners looked at their steel wheat warehouses and instead saw three floating piles of gold. They realized they could dismantle the ships and sell the scrap metal for a significant profit. The only problem was that this violated the terms of their purchase agreement with the US government.

But hey, no risk, no reward! The ships were dismantled and sold for parts and scrap, and Bill and his partners made out like bandits.

About a year later, Bill received a call from the US Maritime Service's Tokyo office, inquiring about the ships' whereabouts.

"Mr. Yuan," the voice on the other end said, "our inspectors couldn't locate the vessels in Taiwan. Is there a mistake?"

Bill replied, "No mistake. I'm scheduled to be in Tokyo soon. Why don't we discuss this in person?"

They met for lunch at a Tokyo hotel on a sweltering summer day. They discussed the missing ships, of course, but Bill remained conspicuously noncommittal about where exactly they were docked. "I'll need to check with my partners," he said. "I'm sure it's just a mix-up."

When they'd finished their meal, the agent excused himself to visit the restroom. Bill took the opportunity to discreetly place $15,000 in the agent's jacket pocket.

When the agent returned, they paid the bill and parted ways with a cordial handshake and Bill's promise to follow up.

Bill hoped he'd heard the last of it.

He hadn't.

A few weeks later, the agent called again, his tone much more pointed than before. "Mr. Yuan, I'll be blunt. I'm afraid $15,000 isn't going to cut it."

"Oh, my apologies," Bill said reassuringly—and with a silent roll of his eyes. "Let's meet again. I know I can make it right."

They met again soon afterward in Tokyo, and Bill passed the agent a briefcase containing an additional $35,000. "Hopefully this makes up for my error and any inconvenience," he said with a smile.

Bill shook the agent's hand and left the meeting, this time certain the matter was resolved.

But once again, he was wrong.

When Bill returned home to the United States, federal officers were there to greet him. He was stunned to learn that his two meetings with the Maritime Service agent were part of a sting operation. His second conversation with the agent had been audio recorded (the agent wore a hidden microphone), and other agents had taken pictures of the two of them throughout the meeting, including the handoff of the $35,000.

The government brought federal charges against Bill and his associates and took him into custody. His business partners, however, were safely tucked away in Taiwan and never returned to the States to face prosecution.

In the absence of the other participants, the government pointed all their cannons at Bill Yuan, with two experienced and respected assistant US attorneys leading the charge. The evidence, including wiretaps, was overwhelming.

I first met Bill soon after the government charged him in the matter. We were introduced at a dinner hosted by Victor Belott, a friend of notorious mob boss Sam DeCavalcante. By the way our mutual friends facilitated the introduction, I understood there was an expectation by all parties that I would represent him.

Despite the severity of the charges, we managed to negotiate a plea deal. Bill pleaded guilty in exchange for a short probationary sentence, and of course the $300,000 bond he had paid upon the purchase of the naval vessels was forfeited.

This whole matter was no doubt an embarrassment for Bill Yuan, but his new criminal record was not the end of him or his business success. As is often the case, even convicted felons have nine lives.

Years after his guilty plea in federal court, Bill was honored by President Jimmy Carter as an outstanding immigrant businessman. He continued his work at his plastics company and his import-export businesses until his death in 2019 at the age of eighty-five.

The thing that has always struck me about representing Bill was learning just how easy it was to effectively *buy* a sitting United States senator. Bill never passed Senator Eastland a briefcase full of cash; he simply lost several card games to him. It was an ingenious way to buy influence because no one could ever prove that Bill was letting Eastland win.

It could all be easily explained away, as Bill had said, as "just the luck of the draw."

Scenes from My Life

Photo shot at Castle Vittoro on October 15, 1940. Jerry Catena, Longhi Zwillman, Doc Stacher, and Richie "The Boot" Boiordo are shown with others.

Chris in his white US Navy uniform in 1956.

Chris in his US Navy hat along his dad in 1957.

Chris, Jimmy Hoffa, and others at a Teamster convention in Atlantic City, circa 1972.

Simone R. "Sam the Plumber" DeCavalcante (right) and S. M. "Chris" Franzblau (left) following DeCavalcante's appearance before the SCI (State Commission of Investigation), 1970.
CREDIT: PRESS PHOTO

Mafia head Gerardo Catena and his attorney S.M. "Chris" Franzblau arrive for an appearance before the SCI (State Commission of Investigation), 1970.

CREDIT: ASSOCIATED PRESS WIREPHOTO

Chris as he's leaning against his red Mercedes in 2024.

Chris out golfing, 2023.

Chris with his dog, circa 2013.

CHAPTER 15

Busted for *Not* Burning Books

Accusing a politician or political party of "book burning" has become a commonly used attack line over the years, going back to Nazi Germany's infamous destruction of banned books in the 1930s. The accusation is that someone who destroys books to get them out of circulation is an enemy of knowledge and competing ideas, someone who wants to control what other people think so they seek and destroy texts with opposing viewpoints.

But the most prolific "book burners" in the world aren't dictators or cult leaders. Instead, it is the publishers themselves who have made the destruction of brand-new, perfect-condition, unread books a huge and highly profitable industry.

Unsurprisingly, it's also an industry the mob has stuck its fingers in as a way to make some easy money.

In 2001, I was introduced to Michael Imposimato, the mastermind behind the appropriately named Book Destruction Company, based out of Irvington, New Jersey. On the surface, this appeared to be a legitimate business providing a necessary service in the publishing industry. But as I would soon learn, Book Destruction Company was enmeshed in corruption and generating enormous profits through their under-the-radar illegal activities.

I was brought in to help Imposimato with what at first seemed to be a straightforward civil case between a publishing house and one of its vendors. I certainly did not expect to learn as much as I did about book destruction as a method of high-stakes deception.

Michael was a sharp, intelligent, self-made man in his midforties, seemingly successful in several business endeavors. The one he seemed to focus on most at the time, though, was his book destruction and disposal business. His right-hand man was Joel Kraemer, a former attorney whom Michael employed as a salesperson and assistant. They worked in a set of beautiful offices overlooking the reservoir on Route 46 in Jersey.

In my initial meeting with the pair, I asked, "So, how exactly does the book destruction process work?"

Michael leaned back and smiled. "It's simple. We handle excess inventory for publishers. They want to maintain market value, so we destroy unsold books to prevent them from flooding secondary markets."

Joel and Michael explained that publishers contracted with them to protect the market value of books by destroying any surplus of printed copies. Destroying the books meant they could not be resold at discounted prices in secondary markets, essentially preventing the devaluation of the product that comes with wholesale distribution.

In the secondary market, wholesalers typically bought overruns and returns to resell to retailers at a discount. There was significant demand for educational texts, coffee table books, research volumes, and novels, and those overruns and returns could be marketed to retail stores such as Borders, Barnes & Noble, and college bookstores. Since the stores bought them at wholesale prices, they could sell the books to customers at deep discounts, 60 percent or more off the retail prices.

When a publishing company like McGraw-Hill sold to retailers such as Borders and Barnes & Noble, they would make sophisticated sales projections—projections that were based on maintaining market pricing for as long as possible. That is, publishers want to charge full price or close to full price for every copy; they don't usually want to see their products hit the stores' bargain bins.

You may ask, "Well, if they're so worried about having overruns, why would they print so many copies of each title?"

Good question.

To ensure they could meet any unexpected demand, the publishers would print overruns beyond their estimates. The cost of these overruns was minimal, as it involved only the cost of paper—the fixed costs of the run had already been covered. McGraw-Hill would then store its overruns in a warehouse in Hightstown, New Jersey. If destruction was necessary, the books were sent to a destruction center in Irvington, New Jersey, which was relatively close to the warehouse.

"How do you ensure the books are actually destroyed?" I probed.

Joel chimed in. "We weigh them before and after transport. It's cost-effective compared to counting every single book. Plus, we provide Affidavits of Destruction."

He went on to explain the protocol for destruction. The books were transported by tractor trailer from the Hightstown warehouse to the Irvington destruction freight platform. The boxes of books were weighed at both Hightstown and Irvington to ensure accuracy. (Weighing was preferred over counting individual books because it was easy, fast, and much cheaper.) To guarantee all books sent from Hightstown were destroyed at the Irvington facility, the weights recorded at each location had to match. The destruction company then certified that there were no discrepancies in the weights and provided an Affidavit of Destruction to McGraw-Hill, assuring the publisher that all the books had been completely destroyed and therefore taken off the market for good, never to be seen, read, or sold again.

It's important to note here that the trailers full of books usually sat unattended for a week or two in a lot adjacent to the loading dock in Irvington before the books were unloaded and destroyed.

It's also helpful to do some quick math. Each trailer contained twenty-five thousand to forty thousand books, which represented enormous wholesale sales value. Even if each book earned a wholesaler a measly two dollars, each truckload represented $50,000 to $80,000 in potential profits for doing nothing but *not* destroying all those books.

You can see how an "industrious" businessperson might see the potential in some of these books *falling off the truck*, so to speak.

That's exactly what McGraw-Hill began to suspect.

As many as 20–30 percent of the books sent for destruction were showing up in a secondary market. They had begun appearing on the shelves at Barnes & Noble and in other retail stores. This resulted in exactly what the publisher wanted to avoid: too much of its product sitting on shelves in the open market, thereby devaluing its product and preventing it from reasonably charging full price for a book that many retailers now had filling up their bargain bins.

McGraw-Hill hired retired New York City Police Department detectives to investigate, but months of surveillance dug up little evidence of wrongdoing. McGraw-Hill then called in the FBI, which traced the books by implanting high-frequency sound-emitting devices in them before they were sent from Hightstown. (Tiny, trackable GPS chips were not an option back then.) When these trackers were found to be moving throughout the retail distribution chain after being dropped off at Irvington, McGraw-Hill had proof that its books were being hijacked and resold rather than being destroyed.

Investigators found that after the books were offloaded and weighed in at Irvington, a substantial number were transferred to a different loading dock in the rear of the book destruction facility. There, the product was sold to various retailers for around 10 percent of the list price in cash.

McGraw-Hill initiated a lawsuit against the Book Destruction Company and its president, Michael Imposimato.

The publisher quickly secured injunctions against the sale of McGraw-Hill books and against Book Destruction Company, suing for both compensatory and punitive damages. The FBI seized several trailer loads of undestroyed books—six trailers in total— found in the Book Destruction Company's lot and emitting the high-frequency sounds used for tracking.

During the depositions I was hired to conduct, we discovered McGraw-Hill books obtained in a secondary market were being refurbished in a Barnes & Noble warehouse in Columbia, Missouri. This prompted the FBI to expand its searches, uncovering similar findings at other locations across the country. It became evident that the retailer had been buying McGraw-Hill books on the secondary market.

Strangely, though, Barnes & Noble was never named as a defendant in the lawsuit.

McGraw-Hill had my client dead to rights, and the civil case was settled quickly. Book Destruction Company agreed to pay $1 million in damages—$100,000 up front and the remaining balance to be paid over the next eighteen years at $50,000 per year. With that agreement, the case was dismissed on the condition that Book Destruction Company would cease operations.

That would have been the end of it, if not for two important events that happened within months of the settlement. First, my client, Michael Imposimato, passed away from cancer, leaving no estate. So, aside from his initial $100,000 payment, McGraw-Hill never received another dime of their $1 million settlement.

Second, months later, a former employee of Book Destruction Company opened a new facility in Brazil, Indiana. It appeared the late Mr. Imposimato's equipment from the Irvington facility had been sold and moved to Indiana, where this new book destruction business was established—this time, however, without McGraw-Hill as a customer.

In no time, books were once again hitting the black market and being resold to distributors at retail bookstores. This led to a second investigation, this time focusing on the president of the new company and the Indiana operation.

As Yogi Berra once said, "It was like déjà vu all over again."

The president of the Indiana company, Robert Baker, retained me to represent him after federal authorities shut down the operation, which had been running for nearly two years. A grand jury was convened, and representatives from the FBI and the US Department of Justice came to New Jersey to meet with me and my client.

I asked Mr. Baker, "You've been offered immunity. Do you have any concerns about testifying?"

He shook his head. "I don't want to be forced to testify against anyone. I'd rather keep my Fifth Amendment rights intact." So my client refused the immunity deal they were offering, which meant there was a real danger of him being sent to prison.

The investigation continued, and Baker was eventually subpoenaed to appear before a grand jury in Kentucky. He and I flew from New Jersey to Nashville, and then drove from Nashville to Louisville for the appearance, although we had made it known my client intended to plead the Fifth for every question.

We arrived at the courthouse on time that morning and sat there almost the entire day, waiting to be called. At 3:00 p.m., the assistant US attorney excused Baker without requiring him to testify. Maybe they had already gotten what they wanted from the others they'd indicted. Or maybe Michael Imposimato's cancer-related death so soon after the end of the previous case made the prosecutors show mercy to my client, who was an older gentleman also suffering from cancer and heart problems. For whatever reason, my client was free to return home.

He never received another summons. They had apparently cut him loose for good.

The others indicted in the illegal sale of books scheduled for destruction all pleaded guilty and received substantial federal prison sentences. My client, Mr. Baker, however, retired quietly at the age of eighty—and presumably paid retail price for his books for the few years he had left to live.

CHAPTER 16

Mounting Lies

Most of my clients, as you've no doubt picked up on, were pretty bad guys.

I know it is hard for many people to understand this, but as a defense attorney, I try not to think of my clients in terms of *good* and *bad*. My responsibilities are the same whether they committed the crimes they're charged with or not. I have a legal and ethical responsibility to defend them vigorously using every available legal means.

It's not my job to prove them innocent.

Criminal law doesn't deal in guilty or innocent. It deals in *guilty* or *not guilty*.

So it's my job to try to win my clients a *not guilty* verdict—or to at least get them the best possible deal in exchange for a guilty plea.

There have been a handful of cases throughout my career, though, when I allowed myself the luxury of truly believing in my client's innocence. It was a rare case in which my client was not a professional criminal with deep mob connections but who was instead the opposite: a good, honest cop who was wrongly accused of a terrible crime. This case stands out in my mind because it perfectly captures the tensions, power struggles, and political corruption that defined the late sixties and seventies.

Sometime around 1969 or 1970, a young, handsome Officer Morello was referred to me for defense against a proposed first-degree homicide indictment. His unit was headed up by a police lieutenant who had been promoted during the reign of the late mayor of Newark, Hugh Addonizio. Addonizio had recently been found guilty of corruption during his administration and subsequently sentenced to prison. (He was the mayor I mentioned in chapter 8 who got tied up in the FBI's secret recordings during the Gyp DeCarlo investigation and subsequent arrests.)

More importantly, the city was still raw and recovering from the terrible 1967 Newark riots, a four-day conflict in the streets that resulted in at least twenty-six deaths and hundreds of injuries in July of that year. Tense race relations had driven the riots, and things only deteriorated in the aftermath as white, middle-class residents moved out of the area and minority residents felt unrepresented in the local government. Discrimination was also a big issue with the primarily white police force in a minority-majority urban community.

Against this backdrop, Newark's Puerto Rican community held its annual Labor Day parade to celebrate Puerto Rican Day in the fall of 1969. A large crowd of up to ten thousand people had gathered in front of the steps at city hall, where the mayor and community leaders traditionally addressed the people gathered.

This big of a crowd—especially mostly made up of members of Newark's different minority populations—was a tricky situation for the local police to handle. Law enforcement was well aware of the racial and ethnic undercurrents of the time, and they were desperate not to see a repeat of the riots from two years prior.

The mounted police were brought in for crowd control. Their stables were located up the hill about half a mile away from city hall, and the unit consisted of ten officers on horseback. The officers approached city hall in a "V" formation once they hit Broad Street, with my client, Officer Morello, leading the point due to his superior horsemanship. The lieutenant in charge trailed closely behind the formation.

In the middle of the parade, at the corner of Halsey and William Streets, a fight broke out involving a middle-aged man who appeared to be intoxicated. Officers from the mounted patrol approached the scuffle, and one of the officers struck the man at the center of the conflict on the head. This man fell to the ground unconscious, and he died at the hospital shortly thereafter.

A grand jury investigation ensued. The lieutenant testified that he had witnessed Morello deliver the fatal blow from his position in the back of the formation, as senior officer to the unit. The nine other officers in the unit stated they did not see the assault, which made the grand jury and prosecutor believe they were trying to protect Morello. Several witnesses from the crowd testified that they saw an officer strike the man, but none could identify who it was.

So there was a dead civilian, witnesses from the crowd who saw an unknown police officer strike the man, no testimony either for or against the accused from the other officers, and the senior officer positively identifying one man as the guilty party.

It didn't look good for Officer Morello.

In our first meeting, Morello sat across from me with desperation in his eyes. "You gotta help me," he pleaded. "The lieutenant . . . he's got it out for me. He's the one who struck that man, not me. I didn't do it, but he's pointing the finger at me to save his own skin. The other guys didn't see it because it happened behind them, where the lieutenant was. But I remember seeing the lieutenant in my peripheral. He had his special blue helmet on, standing out in the crowd like a sore thumb."

The grand jury testimony was done in private, so none of the officers knew what the lieutenant had said about Morello until the time of the actual trial.

Morello took the stand during the trial, denying that he had struck anyone that day. The officers behind him testified that they were preoccupied with managing the crowd and did not see who delivered the blow. There were twenty signed statements from independent witnesses, but none could definitively identify the officer involved. It all came down to the lieutenant's testimony against Morello.

The case had drawn significant media attention, with daily coverage in New York and New Jersey. The outlets reported that, on cross-examination, the civilian witnesses could not describe the color of the helmet worn by the officer who struck the victim.

Then, almost as if by divine intervention, two women who had read the news reports appeared at the courthouse and spoke to me. These women told me they witnessed the entire incident and there was no doubt the victim was clubbed by an officer wearing a unique blue helmet. Of course, I knew only one officer was wearing a blue helmet that day . . . and it wasn't my client.

Morello was telling the truth. The lieutenant really did strike the victim, and now I could prove it.

The former witnesses, including all the officers and the lieutenant, were then removed from the courtroom to ensure each witness could not hear any other witness's testimony. The first of my two new witnesses was called to the stand, and I asked, "The officer you saw strike the victim—what color helmet was he wearing?"

She answered, "Blue. No doubt about it. He was the only one wearing a blue helmet."

She was excused, and the other new witness was brought in. She also testified that the offending officer was wearing a distinctive blue helmet.

Soon after that, the lieutenant was called back to the stand.

"Lieutenant," I said, "I have one last question: What color helmet were you wearing that day?"

Not sensing the trap, he puffed up his chest and proudly answered, "Blue. Only lieutenants and captains can wear blue helmets. Patrolmen wear white."

The prosecution had no further questions.

The jury quickly acquitted my client.

It was a good day.

Officer Morello, disillusioned, retired from the Newark Police Department shortly thereafter, and the mounted police unit was eventually disbanded.

The lieutenant was never prosecuted, investigated, or disciplined.

A small celebration was held after the trial to celebrate Morello's acquittal. My two star witnesses attended, and they shared with me a new detail: They had gone to the prosecutor's office before the trial and reported what they had seen, including the detail about the blue helmet. However, their statements were never presented to the grand jury, nor were they called as witnesses by the prosecution. I never would have known about them if they hadn't sought me out on their own.

I found out later that the investigation had been overseen by the lieutenant himself, with the knowledge of the Newark police chief. So the guilty individual was literally in charge of investigating the crime. No wonder the only two witnesses who could have identified him were suppressed.

Officer Morello's story serves as a reminder that justice is so much more than what occurs in the courtroom. Justice is about uncovering buried truths and the courage it takes to speak up and set the record straight.

Morello's case lingered in my mind for a long time because it represented the very forces I consistently saw at play in my work with the mob. Corruption, manipulation, and wielding power to silence the innocent and protect the guilty—this is exactly what allowed organized crime to endure for so long.

Defending Morello taught me that real victory is not always just about getting a not-guilty verdict.

Sometimes, it really is about bringing the truth to light when it matters most. When you have the right client, it can truly be about proving them innocent.

CHAPTER 17

Always Carry a
Steel Briefcase

In the early 1980s, I represented Sol Rogoff, the president of a once-popular Northeast retail chain of stores called Two Guys (originally known as Two Guys from Harrison). The company started in Harrison, New Jersey, in the midforties and in 1959 merged with the manufacturer of the Vornado line of electronic fans and air conditioners, forming a new company called Vornado, Inc.

Two Guys continued to expand and subsequently grew to more than a hundred locations throughout the Northeast during the sixties and early seventies. Business slowed by the midseventies, however, so Vornado started selling off individual Two Guys locations.

When I was representing Sol Rogoff, things weren't looking good for Two Guys. They were in the midst of negotiations for a takeover by billionaires Steve Roth and David Mandelbaum, who wanted the company not for its retail business but for the prime real estate their stores sat on in New Jersey and New York.

The CEO of Two Guys was a New York attorney named Fred Zissu, who was also the executor of the estates of the company's original owners and stockholders. As part of the probate case between the original Two Guys owners and Vornado, my client, Rogoff, was subpoenaed to testify before a US Senate committee in Washington, DC. After a few postponements due to Rogoff's poor health, we were finally committed to appear before the committee on the Tuesday before Thanksgiving. We flew down early in the morning with plans to return that same day on an 8:00 p.m. flight to Newark from Dulles Airport.

If this story seems boring so far, don't worry. It's about to pick up.

The hearings on Capitol Hill ended at about 4:00 p.m., and Sol and I had planned to have an early dinner at the Palm Steak House about ten blocks from the Capitol building—an easy walk. Or so we thought.

As we walked past some brownstones in one of the DC metro neighborhoods, three young men appeared out of nowhere behind us and made their presence known.

"Freeze!" one of them yelled. "Give us whatever you've got in your pockets!"

I was around fifty years old at the time—certainly not a young man, but I wasn't entirely helpless either. Besides, I'd spent nearly every day of the past twenty years working with professional gangsters by this point. Three kids with obviously knocking knees weren't quite enough to scare me.

We were on the sidewalk with the brownstones on one side and a line of parked cars on the other. I instinctively pushed Sol between two parked cars and told him to run. He took off down the center of the street. One mugger broke off to chase him, leaving his two friends to take care of me.

I tightened my grip on the handle of the steel-frame briefcase in my hand and locked eyes with the attacker nearest me.

He pulled a knife from his jacket and took a step toward me, pointing the blade at my body. He was so sure he'd found himself an easy target in an expensive suit and full pockets that he never saw my briefcase coming.

The steel corner caught him on the side of the head. He hit the pavement.

His friend stood there stunned for a split second before reaching into his pocket and retrieving his switchblade. He came at me and was greeted with the opposite corner of my briefcase. I caught him square in the face. He stumbled backward, looked down at his semiconscious partner sprawled on the sidewalk, and decided he'd had enough. He cursed at me, turned, and ran the opposite direction.

My heart was racing. It had all happened so quickly, but I'd managed to fight off two of our three attackers! But what about Sol?

I took off running down the sidewalk to find Sol and caught up to him at the corner of the next block. He said the guy chasing him disappeared once they got to a more crowded area.

Shaking, sweating, and feeling all the adrenaline quickly exiting my bloodstream, I sat down with Sol Rogoff at the Palm and enjoyed the most satisfying steak dinner of my life.

Two days later, my Thanksgiving dinner was interrupted by a phone call from Sol. He told me he was celebrating Thanksgiving at the home of his cousin, Bernie Edelstein, a major Teamsters Union official— and the man who nominated Jimmy Hoffa to his first presidency of the International Brotherhood of Teamsters. Edelstein was also a notorious character who was later forced out of the Teamsters following their investigations into Hoffa's subsequent disappearance. He was one of my clients.

Sol explained that over dinner, he shared with Edelstein what happened earlier that week in DC. Less than a minute into the phone call, though, Edelstein grabbed the phone from Sol and told me the rest of the story.

"Chris!" he blurted out excitedly. "Sol was telling me what happened to him in DC. He said he and his lawyer got mugged, but his lawyer took out two of the goons with his briefcase. I stopped him right there and said, 'Hey, Sol, was your attorney from New Jersey?' When he said yes, I knew exactly who he was talking about. I told him, 'It was Chris Franzblau, wasn't it? He's the only lawyer in Jersey who would react that way!'"

Every trial lawyer dreams of developing a reputation as a fighter in the courtroom. But this was one of a handful of times throughout my career when it was a fight *outside* the courtroom that really cemented my rep as a tough lawyer within New Jersey's mob culture.

CHAPTER 18

The First Jersey
Securities Boys

In the mideighties, I was hired to represent one of the defendants in a massive tax fraud case that *might* have been . . . shall we say . . . *mob-adjacent*. I say *adjacent* because it wasn't technically a mob case, although the principal player in the case was someone who was widely speculated to have been connected to some known figures in organized crime (although this was never proven).

Gene Mulvihill became a legendary figure in New Jersey's resort business in the seventies and eighties. He was known as an "idea man," always coming up with one wild business idea after another.

His exploits made himself and several other people a whole lot of money.

They also *cost* several people a lot of money—and in a few cases, their lives.

Mulvihill and his business partner, Robert Brennan, were the founders of First Jersey Securities, one of the original penny stock securities companies that peddled worthless stock to gullible investors who'd get hoodwinked by a too-good-to-be-true sales pitch. The operation was built on a glitzy advertising campaign in which Brennan emerged from a helicopter and enticed potential investors to "Come Grow with Us."

The only ones who grew any real wealth through First Jersey Securities were its owners—namely, Mulvihill and Brennan. The outfit was a classic predatory "pump and dump" operation in which high-pressure salespeople sold stock in worthless companies that First Jersey fraudulently promoted. At its peak, First Jersey employed more than twelve hundred people and generated more than $75 million a year in profits. Brennan and Mulvihill rode this wave for a while until the Securities and Exchange Commission (SEC) charged First Jersey Securities with swindling investors out of more than $300 million. Brennan eventually agreed to pay $100 million to settle the charges.

In another one of Brennan and Mulvihill's notorious deals, the pair came up $100,000 short and went to their high school buddy John Steinbach for help finding an investor to fork over the cash they needed in exchange for a share of ownership. Steinbach just happened to be the stepson of my longtime associate Abner "Longie" Zwillman, who had a long and rich history in organized crime stretching back to New Jersey's illegal Prohibition era speakeasies.

Steinbach connected Brennan and Mulvihill to the owner of a garbage collection company, who bought a hundred thousand shares of their new business for the $100,000 they needed. A month later, this new investor and partial owner dropped dead.

Interesting timing.

Brennan held on to the late garbage man's shares and hid his investment from his other investors under a "street name" as their company—the ironically named *Fidelity Investment*—grew in value. He played a cat-and-mouse game with the SEC for years, being found guilty of securities fraud in the nineties and later convicted of money laundering and bankruptcy fraud in 2001, which put him behind bars for almost a decade.

While Brennan was playing a never-ending game of financial hide-and-seek with the SEC, his longtime business partner, Gene Mulvihill, was getting rich running a series of schemes in the burgeoning New Jersey gaming and resort industry. When the opportunity arose for Mulvihill to purchase the Vernon Valley / Great Gorge golf and ski resort in Vernon Township, New Jersey—also home to the local Playboy Club— he turned back to his old friend John Steinbach for another infusion of cash.

Steinbach's notorious stepfather, Longie Zwillman, had died by then and had left all his money to his wife. She remarried, and her new husband lost nearly all that inheritance on a failed professional football league. By the time Steinbach's mother died, leaving everything to him, there was only $600,000 of Zwillman's multimillion-dollar fortune left.

Steinbach gave all of it to Mulvihill to finance the acquisition of Great Gorge. What happened there over the next eighteen years became the stuff of New Jersey legend.

Mulvihill went all in on developing Great Gorge and Vernon Valley as a premier vacation destination, trying through sheer force of will to turn it into the Orlando of the Northeast. The golf resort eventually went bankrupt, but Mulvihill had a new obsession by then: his much-beloved and much-maligned amusement park, Action Park.

Action Park began as a way for Mulvihill to make some summer cash during the ski resort's offseason. In 1976, he installed a dangerously steep (and structurally unsound) alpine slide, followed by two water slides and a go-kart track in 1978. By the time it was shut down in 1996, it had grown into a major destination with more than seventy attractions—a mix of water slides, boat rides, pool attractions, and motor sports spread out across a sprawling two-hundred-and-fifty-acre plot of New Jersey swampland and ski slopes.

On the surface, Action Park seemed like a huge success. But anyone who took even a cursory look behind the exciting Action Park TV commercials and into Mulvihill's shady business dealings could see the bodies piling up.

Literally.

Action Park was widely (and fairly) considered to be the most dangerous amusement park in the country. Dozens—sometimes hundreds—of people left the park every single day with serious injuries. The rides were built with practically zero regard for engineering principles, and many were invented by Mulvihill himself—including the Cannonball Loop, a water slide that ended in a loop-the-loop that Mulvihill reportedly sketched on the back of a napkin and handed to someone to make for him. According to the 2023 documentary film *Class Action Park*, the first test dummies thrown down the slide came out the other end in pieces. After many tweaks, Mulvihill started testing the ride with human test dummies—namely, any of his teenaged employees who were dumb enough to try it out. When the kids shot out the bottom of the slide—bruised, bloody, semiconscious, and missing teeth—they'd be congratulated by their friendly "Uncle Gene," who'd smile and hand them a crisp $100 bill for their courage.

Action Park became a rite of passage for Jersey kids in the eighties and nineties. Students would start the school year comparing scars and sharing battle stories from their summer adventures falling off different rides, flipping a go-kart at fifty miles per hour, or nearly getting decapitated by the rotors of a runaway speed boat.

But not everyone made it back home from Action Park. There were a total of six fatalities from park-related accidents between 1980 and the park's closure in 1996.

Despite the trails of blood that were constantly being sprayed off the sidewalks, none of these injuries was ever reported to the state. The state agencies required the park to report any "serious injuries," but it foolishly allowed the park itself to determine what made an injury "serious." Mulvihill's team, then, decided an injury was serious only if the person left the park strapped to a board in the back of an ambulance. Those figures were still unusually high, but it allowed Action Park to stay open despite the growing number of parents who were tired of seeing their children come home limping.

Plenty of those families sued Mulvihill, including the parents of nineteen-year-old George Larsson Jr., who became Action Park's first fatality in 1980 when he flew off the Alpine Slide and crashed into nearby rocks. Despite the lawsuits and outcries, Mulvihill maintained a firm "never settle" policy and required every case against him to go all the way to court. This weeded out the vast majority of complainants and eventually even prevented lawyers from wanting to represent someone against Action Park. There just wasn't enough money in it for them.

Why would Mulvihill fight so hard against seemingly legitimate injury claims? Because despite clear state guidelines requiring it, Action Park had no insurance.

None.

At all.

Instead of getting actual coverage like he was required to do, Mulvihill created a phony insurance company and wrote himself a fake policy to fool the state. And since he had this perfectly good business entity on the books, why not also use it to launder money for his other businesses?

When enough of Gene Mulvihill's illegal activities finally came to light, he and several of his employees were indicted on tax fraud. One of those employees was Mulvihill's personal assistant (and girlfriend), who hired me to defend her separately from Mulvihill. I successfully negotiated a plea deal for her, arguing that Mulvihill was clearly the brains and driving force of the entire enterprise, and he'd simply ensnared my client in his enormous web of charm and deception. He pleaded guilty and got a suspended sentence and substantial fines, and my client was given pretrial relief and the indictment was dismissed against her.

Mulvihill was extremely bright and charismatic, and I could understand how he managed to talk so many people into so many stupid things. But the man had no business scruples whatsoever. He didn't think the law applied to him, and he thumbed his nose at anyone who tried to make him play by the rules.

Nonetheless, even after all the lawsuits, convictions, injuries, and even the deaths he was blamed for, New Jersey politicians and businesspeople alike gushed about his genius and business acumen when he died in 2012. Governor Chris Christie himself remarked, "Gene Mulvihill's contributions to the economic development of Sussex County are unquestionable. His unique vision and entrepreneurial spirit will be greatly missed."

That's high praise for someone with such a long history of fraud, illegal business dealings, and likely associations with organized crime. I think it's fair to say that not all the people I've known or worked with over the years have been remembered quite so fondly as Gene Mulvihill.

CHAPTER 19

The Power of the Mob

It's true that I've spent much of my career representing some people who were . . . *not so nice.* I
knew who these guys were, what they did, and what
they were accused of. Other people had some pretty
rough experiences with them. I, however, got along
just fine with most of them. I did my job and represented them to the best of my ability under the law,
and they were appreciative. Sometimes, in fact, those
connections I made in the mob came in kind of handy.

For example, a longtime client of mine was one
of the leading car dealers in New Jersey. He found
out late in the process that a competitor was not only
planning to move into his area but that he'd already
signed a contract to buy an existing dealership nearby.

Tony Pro was the most "connected" guy I knew who operated in the area, so I called in a favor.

"A friend of mine wants to buy that dealership," I told Tony. "Any chance you could 'help' that other buyer's deal fall through?"

"No problem." Tony Pro knew I was representing Jerry Catena, the head of the family, so he was more than happy to help me out.

In no time, we got word that the other buyer's deal *somehow* broke down.

My friend and I worked quickly to draw up a sales contract between him and the existing owner. The sale closed on a Thursday morning, and I left later that afternoon for a family vacation with my wife and kids to Paradise Island in the Bahamas.

The next morning, my vacation was interrupted by a panicked phone call from my friend.

"Chris," he said, "I got to my new dealership this morning ready to hit the ground running. I've got big plans for this place. But a 'business agent' from the Teamsters Union just walked into my office. He introduced himself and said, 'I represent the union workers of this establishment.' I told him that we didn't *have* a union. He slammed a gun down on my desk in front of me and said, '*Now you do.*' What am I supposed to do now?"

This wasn't the first time I'd heard of the Teamsters using strong-arm tactics to force unions into local businesses. It was, unfortunately, all part of the game in the Jersey business community.

Good thing I knew how to play the game.

I said, "Calm down, it's going to be okay. Why don't you and your family fly down here to meet me in the Bahamas? It'll get you out of town for a few days, and our wives and kids can hang out while you and I decide what to do."

He arrived the next day, Saturday, and I spent the weekend trying to reassure him that everything would work out. We decided we'd enjoy a couple of days in paradise, and then we'd leave our families there while he and I flew back to New Jersey on Monday to take care of the Teamster situation.

When we landed in Newark, I called Tony Pro and told him I needed to see him ASAP. He was at his home in Clifton, so my friend and I hopped in a car and were there within the hour.

Tony Pro welcomed us into his home—cordial as always—and listened as we explained the situation. Tony nodded along as my friend told him about the gun-toting union rep's "sales pitch."

When he finished the story, I looked Tony Pro in the eye and said, "So, can you help us out?"

The response was short, immediate, and certain. "Consider it done."

With one call from Tony Pro to the local Teamsters Union agent, the situation was resolved. Forever. My friend operated his dealership—without a union—for decades after, and he never heard from that or any other Teamster business agent again.

It always amazes me how powerful a single phone call from the right person can be. In those circles at that time, Tony Pro and Jerry Catena's words were law, and everyone knew it. This was just one of many times over the years when I really saw how far and how deep the mob's power and influence ran in the Jersey business scene.

• • •

Although representing Hy Chuven in 1962 was my first introduction to the world of organized crime (chapter 2), it was representing Local 560 that propelled me into the national scene. As a young lawyer in my thirties, I was representing the key figures in organized crime who were making headlines, rubbing shoulders with well-known union figures such as Jimmy Hoffa, and having the occasional run-in with celebrities (or at least, as with Sinatra, their closed dressing room doors).

It was exhilarating. For the first time, I understood the lure of the celebrity spotlight—and why people were willing to go to such great lengths to hold on to it.

Considering the atrocities mobsters committed back then, it is easy to wonder why they were treated so well and why their criminal lifestyles were so glamorized. I get that. But there was something indescribable in these encounters. These guys had a *gravitational pull* that drew people into their orbit. I admit that I got caught up in it myself. I enjoyed the access, the power, and the special treatment that came with standing beside these strangely likable men who were doing unthinkably terrible things.

The fifteen years I spent representing Local 560 gave me a real lesson in American history that I wasn't taught in school. It showed me that the mob was embedded into the very fabric of everyday life.

My eyes were opened to the way the mob financed its illegal activity with endless funds from union pensions; how the mob's control over labor unions resulted in sweetheart deals for those companies that were willing to pay off the right people;

and how virtually every business in the United States was directly or indirectly affected by the mob's total control of the Teamsters Union, whose truck driver members were essential in transporting pretty much every type of goods.

After my experience representing Local 560, Tony Pro, and Sally Bugs, I never wanted to go back to a "normal" law practice. Thanks to Jerry Catena and others, I didn't have to. I got to stay involved in that fascinating world for most of my career.

In that time, I saw mob bosses rise and fall.

I saw untouchable men convicted and imprisoned.

I saw dangerous men disappear forever.

I fought to defend the rights of criminals.

I stood side by side with some of the country's most notorious gangsters, extortionists, racketeers, and even killers—in court, at weddings, and at funerals.

I celebrated the births of their children.

I mourned their loss when they died.

And now, at ninety-four, I may very well be the last of that entire "connected" generation.

The last man standing.

The last mob lawyer.

ACKNOWLEDGMENTS

I want to thank Allen Harris and Michael Levin for providing insights and assistance writing and editing, and for helping me get the book to the end zone. I also owe a debt of gratitude to my buddies Septic, Stevie, and R.C. Cola for publishing books and providing inspiration to finally get this book written!